. D

INDIAN RELICS OF THE PACIFIC NORTHWEST

N. G. *Seaman*

INDIAN RELICS

OF THE

PACIFIC NORTHWEST

BINFORDS & MORT, *Publishers*

Portland   ·   Oregon   ·   97242

LIBRARY OF CONGRESS CATALOG CARD NUMBER: 66-28021
CLOTH EDITION: ISBN: 0-8323-0132-9
PAPER EDITION: ISBN: 0-8323-0236-8
741-4PIC

Printed in the United States of America

SECOND EDITION
Second Printing 1974

CONTENTS

INTRODUCTION

When people leave behind them a writing on any subject with the idea and hope that it may be read with interest, it seems right that the reader should know the background of the writer, so that proper judgment can be passed on opinions given.

I am not writing as an authority on the subject of Indian relics. Indeed, I wish I knew of some such person who could answer the many questions that continue to arise in my own mind. If there is value in this writing, it may be largely in bringing to the thought of others the numerous "don't knows" that I have encountered so that they, in turn, may seek the answers.

Naturally I have read what could be found on stone-age relics, and no doubt I have been influenced by these readings; but it has been my intention to confine this book, as much as possible, to my own observations, and to what I have learned from my old Indian friends—as I feel that it is of more value to record a little knowledge from difficult sources, or from close study, than a book full from other people's works.

I have, therefore, confined my writing to my own hunting grounds, which have been Oregon, much of Washington, and part of Northern California.

For most of my life I have been interested in Indian artifacts; and have been collecting them for much of that time. In my later explorations I have had the companionship of my two nephews, C. L. Marshall and Earl A. Marshall, who went on their first relic hunt with me when they were about big enough to carry one fishing sinker. Our profession of civil engineering added to our opportunity to be outside.

My good friend Robert H. Miller, who wrote the section on the "Bead Patch," has accompanied me on many of my collecting jaunts. He was once quite a hunter and fisherman. Then, one day, while trolling for salmon along Sauvies Island, he became disgusted with fish that would not bite, so he pulled ashore on the island and was walking up the beach when he found an arrowhead. That was about the end of his fishing days. The lure of hunting for relics was far stronger than for ducks, pheasants, or fish. His very large collection shows how persistently he followed his new interest.

Another helpful friend was Lieutenant Colonel O. S. M. Mc-Cleary; during his long service in the army, he was stationed at many points in the West and early acquired an interest in the Indians and their stone relics.

To Peter Binford, founder of Binfords & Mort, Publishers, I am especially grateful for his keeping after me until I finally got the material ready for publication; also to my many old Indian friends who supplied me with the remembered but heretofore unrecorded information about the use of various artifacts. Among these were notably Bill Charley of Celilo; Louie Brown, an interpreter for the Yakimas; Pipe Shear of Satus Canyon; We-la-lu-tum of the Wascos; and Albert Kokup and Tulux Holliquilla of Warm Springs.

Unfortunately the best days are past for the amateur hunter of stone-age relics. Not only have more and more hobbyists turned to the field, but waters of the huge reservoirs behind the dams are fast drowning out the old Indian sites. However, it is easy to believe that, as long as the river winds blow, occasional sand bars will be eroded to reveal their dormant treasures. Dry caves of the desert country likely still conceal many desirable artifacts, and old desert lake beds should hold many clues to native life there when the area was habitable by man.

In *Indian Relics of the Pacific Northwest*, I have done my best to answer often-asked questions about the relics and give a picture of the hunting grounds as they now are and as they were years ago; also to include other incidents of Indian life that I hope may be of interest. Perhaps the book will, in a measure, pay my debt to this region for the many trips I have enjoyed to different parts, and particularly for my searches of the banks of the Columbia River before any dams destroyed the old camp sites. The Columbia is one of the grand rivers of the world—when the wind doesn't blow.

N. G. Seaman

INDIAN RELICS OF THE PACIFIC NORTHWEST

Indians near The Dalles left many records in stone.

Part One

THE INDIANS

WITHIN THE BOUNDARIES OF THE PACIFIC NORTHWEST THERE were many separate Indian tribes, speaking their own language and having their own methods of transportation, food supply, and housing. In many regions there is evidence of numerous successive cultures. Surviving the wear of centuries on canyon walls and cliffs are rude designs daubed in red ochre or outlined in primitive carving.

Along the basalt walls of the Columbia River and in the desert country east of the Cascades are countless delineations of hunters, deer, sunbursts, owls, and strange configurations—all attesting that primordial man once passed here.

The origins, use, and meanings of these picture writings and rock carvings are still a mystery, and they are not explained either by the Indians or by the anthropologists and archeologists. Studies do indicate, though, that the culture of the early peoples did somewhat resemble that of historic Indians. These researches, moreover, have furnished additional evidence to support the theory of the Asiatic origin of the Indian.

Remains of later periods are much more numerous, and considerable progress is being made in collecting and preserving them. I am not an authority on Indian relics but I have spent over half a century hunting them. Beneath layers of lava and volcanic ash, stone and obsidian weapons and bone fragments have been found. In Oregon, the Linn County mounds, the Deschutes region, the Malheur and Catlow caves, and a great many other sites have yielded weapons, utensils, and tools of the Indians.

Burial mounds in irregular patterns mark the places where the dead, with their crude artifacts, lie buried. Along the coast, kitchen middens—heaps of shells, bone, and stone fragments, and miscellaneous refuse, overgrown with grass and trees—indicate the existence of prehistoric homes. Where the Coast Highway cuts through such a kitchen midden, as it does in several places, varying levels or strata in the heap are revealed, denoting successive occupations of the locality.

Archeological research, though, has merely scratched the surface in many areas such as the Yakima River basin, the Puget Sound region, and Pacific County in southwest Washington.

The Tribes

At the time of the arrival of the first white men, the Chinooks held sway along the Columbia from its mouth to the Cascades. Related to the Chinooks were the Clatsops, who occupied the south side of the river up to Tongue Point and along the coast to Tillamook Head. Also related to the Chinooks were the Cathlamets, who dwelt a short distance farther up the river near Knappa. Numerous bands on Sauvies Island and about the mouth of the Willamette were known by the collective name of Multnomahs. The Clackamas tribe lived in the Clackamas Valley and about the falls of the Willamette. In all, some thirty-six tribes of the Chinookan family dwelt on the south shore of the Columbia, and as many others dwelt on the Washington side.

The Athapascans occupied two widely separated regions. On the Clatskanie and upper Nehalem rivers lived the Tlatskanai, a warlike tribe. It is said that the early Hudson's Bay Company trappers did not dare to traverse their lands in a group of fewer than sixty armed men. In southwestern Oregon dwelt the other Athapascans—the Tututni, the Upper Coquilles, the Chasta-costas, and the Chetcoes. Also in this southwestern region were the Umpquas and the Siuslaws, who together form a separate family.

The Salishan, or Salish, family was widely divided, with tribes in western Montana, in the northern portions of Idaho and Washington, and a small stock around Tillamook and Nehalem bays and along the Siletz River in Oregon. All spoke a similar language.

Established in 1825, Vancouver on the Columbia was the chief central fort of the great Hudson's Bay Company. The Indians shown here probably came as traders.

The Wascopam Mission at The Dalles of the Columbia was built in 1838. Here in the spring of 1840, several hundred Indians were baptized, following a weeklong camp meeting.

One of the most important families was the Calapooian. This numerous people occupied the whole of the Willamette Valley above the falls, practiced flattening of the head, and lived on game and roots. A dozen tribes of this family inhabited the Willamette region at the coming of the white man. The Atfalati or Tualati, numbering more than thirty bands, occupied the beautiful and fertile Tualatin Valley. Other tribes of this group were the Yamhills, the Chemeketas, and the Santiams.

The southern part of Oregon was occupied by divisions of three families: the powerful Klamath and Modoc tribes of the Lutuamians or Sahaptians, the Takelmans of the upper Rogue River, and two "spill-overs" from California—the Shastas and Karoks of the Hokan family.

The upper Columbia River country was the home of other Sahaptians. The greater part of this family lived in eastern Washington and the Lewis River district of Idaho, and included, among others, the Nez Perce, the Palouse, the Walla Walla, the Yakima, and the Colville. Four of the tribes—the Willewah branch of the Nez Perces, the Umatillas, the Teninos of the Deschutes River, and the Tyghs of the Tygh Valley, inhabited the uplands of central and eastern Oregon. The Waiilatpuan branch was represented by the powerful Cayuse or "horse" Indians, dwelling on the headwaters of the Umatilla, the Walla Walla, and the Grande Ronde rivers. A small offshoot of this branch had in times past wandered over the Cascades into western Oregon, and under the name of Molallas lived along the Molalla River. Over the high desert country of the southeastern region roamed the nomadic Snake and Paiute tribes of the Shoshones.

Frequently northern Indians, from the region that is now British Columbia and southeastern Alaska, journeyed south in their war canoes, through the protected Inland Passage, to attack the Puget Sound Indians for the purpose of capturing slaves; and these onslaughts resulted in a transfer of culture. Some interchange also took place between inhabitants of the Columbia River region and those of the Rocky Mountain and Plains areas.

Though there were many separate linguistic groups, such as the Makah and the Puget Sound groups to the north, and the Chinook along the Columbia; and though there were many subdivisions of these groups, the Northwest Indians may generally be divided into two major types, on the basis of culture traits. One comprised those bands east of the Cascade Range, and the other those west of it. The sharp cultural differences that developed between these groups arose in large measure from the barrier to intercourse formed by these lofty mountains. Contributing also to the formation of distinctive culture patterns was the sharp contrast in the physical character and climatic conditions of the two areas. East of the Cascades, in the semiarid plateaus and grasslands of the Columbia River system, considerable cultural similarity existed.

West of the Cascades

West of the mountains to the coast is the rainy section, giving the area the reputation of being wet. It was mostly heavy timber and brush, and from British Columbia south to the Umpqua River in Oregon, native cultures were sufficiently homogeneous to permit this region to be regarded as a single culture area.

The local customs of Indians in the western valleys and coast region differed greatly from those of the interior. The western tribes, because of the density of the forests, usually traveled by canoe. They did not use horses as the dense woods made them undesirable. Trails would have to be cleared for them, and this would be no small task where windfalls might be from four to eight feet in diameter.

There was but little in the big timber that was of use to an Indian. All game preferred the burns or open country. Some years back, before the great forests of Douglas fir were cut, it was possible to travel all day in their darkness and see perhaps only a couple of snakes, a few toads or frogs, and occasionally hear a wren singing. When one came out into a burn, it teemed with life.

Salmon, the most important food of the western tribes, could be taken almost any-where up and down the Columbia, but the best places were the rapids and falls. There the fish would rest in the eddies below the falling waters, becoming easy prey to even the thrust of a spear.

Relics found in the hills where ranches have been cleared, away from the streams, show that Indians have hunted there, or gone there in search of hazelnuts or berries. But the mountains and hills produce few relics, generally speaking, as trips to them—even the regular pilgrimages for huckleberries—did not necessitate the carrying of heavier implements. Knives, scrapers, and arrows were about all they needed.

The most important food of the western tribes was salmon, which they caught in their primitive weirs and traps. The opening of the salmon season in June was attended with great formality. The first salmon caught was sacred, and was eaten ceremonially in a long-established ritual intended to propitiate the salmon and insure future runs. Halibut, cod, shellfish, sturgeon, and fresh-water fish were also widely used. But for Indians on both sides of the Cascades, fish was a major food item. Most bands of Indians lived near enough to the rivers to keep supplied with it.

Game of many kinds, especially deer, elk, and wild fowl, was obtainable throughout the area. Another important food was roots, especially the root of camas, which grew in the grasslands and lowlands. Agriculture was unknown, but seeds and roots were, in fact, the staple food for some bands. Near the Cascades and in the northern highlands, berries, especially huckleberries, were widely used, and small game and deer were hunted. Usually the food was boiled in watertight baskets with hot stones, but some of it, especially roots, was baked over heated rocks.

Clothing was, in the main, fairly well standardized among the western tribes, though there were differences owing to changes in the weather or indicating social status. In mild seasons men wore either nothing or a robe or blanket thrown over the back and fastened across the chest with a string; they also had buckskin shirts, belts, breechcloths, leggings, moccasins, and basketry hats. The basic dress for women was a sort of petticoat, usually made of twisted strings of cedar bark or grass, fastened to a cord or band around the waist and falling to the knees. Occasionally wool was used. Additional garments were worn in

A Chinook mother and child. The Chinooks of the Lower Columbia were sometimes called Flatheads, but this process of flattening the heads of infants was reserved for the nobility. The baby was held in this vise-like headpiece for from three months to a year.

cold and rainy weather. Upper-class women of some bands also wore woven or skin shirts or capes. Tattooing was more common among women than men, but it was usually limited to a few lines or dots on the arms and legs. The face was rarely, if ever, marked. Among some bands, especially those of the lower Columbia, heads were flattened in infancy.

One interesting theory advanced regarding the process of head-flattening is that it originated in the idea that it was unbecoming the dignity of a master to have the same appearance as a slave. Furthermore, since clothing and other insignia were perishable, there might be a mix-up in the next world and the slave be mistaken for a master, enjoying all the privileges of that class. Such a dilemma could not occur if the master were marked indelibly, as in head-flattening. It is interesting to note that, in this process, the infant experienced no unusual pain, nor was the child affected mentally or emotionally by it in later years.

During the summer, the Indians did much moving about from camp to camp; often they would not be home longer than a week or so between camping trips. For these trips all they needed was a simple shelter. They put up a few poles and covered them with mats. But for the winter, when the weather was cold and rainy for long periods, permanent houses were built.

The houses of the western tribes were pretty well standardized and were of a communal type. Cedar planks, two or three feet wide and from three to six inches thick, were cut with wedges of elk-horn or wood, or with chisels of beaver teeth and stone. From these planks and from logs, rectangular houses— forty to a hundred feet or more in length and fourteen to twenty feet wide—were built. The great lodges were roofed over with bark or boards; and along the middle of the floor ran a firepit, the smoke escaping through a gap left along the ridgepole of the roof. The only other opening was a single door.

These longhouses accommodated a number of families, each with its own small fire in the firepit. Bunks lined the walls, and the four or five feet of earthen floor between them and the fire was the living space of each family.

Men, women, children, and dogs mingled in the dusky interior. The houses were put together with lashings; and when fleas and other vermin became intolerable, the houses were dismantled and the planks removed to a new location, supposedly leaving the fleas behind.

Western Crafts

Among these Indians, a h i g h level of technique was achieved in the crafts. The hides of animals, both large and small, were tanned with the hair on; and from these, various articles, such as moccasins, skirts, and drums, were made with considerable skill. Woodworking was in an early stage of development. Though the forms were broadly similar to those used by the Indians farther north, they lacked the technical and artistic skill achieved there. Perhaps the best example of the woodwork of the region was the dugout cedar canoe.

The Indians of river and coast were skilled in fashioning canoes. Each of these was made from a single log, their size varying from the small craft capable of sustaining only one person to the great war canoe in which as many as sixty warriors might safely put to sea. For these graceful vessels, cedar and spruce were usually preferred, though fir was also used.

The native bow, like the canoe, was beautifully and skillfully formed. It was generally made of yew or crabapple wood. The string was a piece of dried seal-gut or deer-sinew, or consisted of twisted bark. The arrows, about a yard long, were made of arrow-wood or cedar. Household utensils included baskets of cedar root fiber or tough grasses often woven so closely as to be watertight, and stone mortars and pestles for pulverizing seeds and wild grains. The principal art displayed was in the carvings on house posts and canoe figureheads, and in the fashioning of woven mats and baskets. Basketry was a highly developed art, many examples of which, richly colored with intricate and pleasing designs, today grace museums or are offered for sale in Indian curio stores.

The hair of dogs, shredded bark, the fur of bears, and the wool of mountain goats were woven on looms made of two uprights connected by rollers at top and bottom. The Indians of Juan de Fuca Strait region were famous for their dog-hair blankets. Some of their articles were skillfully colored with vegetable dyes; reds, yellows, greens, and black being most prevalent. Mats were generally woven from cedar bark and dried rushes, and baskets for many uses were twined from fine roots and grasses. Pottery was unknown, although some stone carving existed before white men came.

To a limited extent, the crafts, especially basketry and wood carving, are still practiced, but almost entirely for the tourist trade, the original motive for such work having been largely eliminated by the introduction of machine-made goods. Baskets, rich in color and design, represent the most highly developed phase of Indian art in the coastal regions. Today, as in the past, grasses, cedar and spruce roots, willows, and straw are the materials most commonly used, with thread, string, and animal hair often woven in as decoration. The weaves have great variety— hard and soft coil, turned and open twine, straight and crossed warps, hemstitching, and imbrication. Skill is also displayed in the working out of color patterns and in the many shapes of the baskets. Curios made by the Indians for tourist trade are sometimes authentic in detail, such as the small model canoes; but the miniature totem poles that some carve are mere imitations of the genuine totem art common to the tribes of Alaska and parts of British Columbia.

East of the Cascades

Approximately two thirds of Washington, east of the Cascades, is occupied by Indians having a "basin" type of culture. The introduction of the horse, shortly before the arrival of the explorers, led to complications and change in the economic life of the natives and to a rapid spread of material cultural elements associated with the horse and with the new mode of life. The Indians of eastern Washington wandered in bands, the range of their wanderings and the size of the bands depending largely on the nature of their food. Because of their nomadic life, the general dwelling was a mat lodge, which could be transported from place to place. Usually, this lodge, a single large room, was rectangular in shape, twenty to sixty feet in length and about sixteen feet in width. Occasionally, the lodges were circular. They were made by weaving mats of tule or cattail and wrapping them about a framework of poles. Two to eight families might live in one lodge.

The underground dwelling was probably known throughout the region, but it seems to have been utilized by relatively few bands; the semi-subterranean dwelling consisted of a circular pit from four to six feet in depth and from ten to fifteen feet in diameter. Surmounting it was a flat or conical roof of sod, supported by planks and matting. Mat houses are rather rare now and are used mostly when Indians are stopping temporarily at some place. The influence of the plains tribes and of the whites is seen in the increased use of skin and canvas tepees and, in some sections, of log cabins.

While a friend and I were setting up our camera to photograph the small hut shown here, a half dozen different Indians raised the flap and took a look at us and then went back in. Finally a tall, middle-aged woman looked at us for a few moments, then came straight for us.

(I was reminded of the time this same companion and I tried to photograph a young Indian woman on horseback, whom we met on a trail along the river. We didn't get the picture, but we did some darting to avoid the pony, got a couple of slashes from a quirt, and heard some vituperous language which we fully understood although we did not know the words. We concluded that not all Indians wanted their pictures taken.)

Now, watching the Indian woman coming so fast, my friend said, "That old girl looks like she's on the warpath; it's me for the top of the cliff. Keep between her and the camera—if you have to, grab it and make the big run."

When the Indian got about ten feet from us, she suddenly stopped still and said,

"How much you charge picture?" That was different. We talked with her a while, got her name, and told her to inquire

This small mat house, about twenty-five feet in diameter, was standing in a low sandy pit near Roosevelt, Washington.

This larger mat house is from the Umatilla country in Oregon, and shows how the larger houses were built.

at the post office in two weeks. As the package didn't come back to us, we feel sure the lady got the picture of her house.

These Indians did not develop a high degree of skill in the crafts except in the making of skin clothes and in basketry. Utensils, such as spoons, dishes, and bowls, were made of wood, but because of the scarcity of timber in the greater part of this area, little artistry in woodworking developed. Canoes, used infrequently, were only rude dugouts. Certain tribes, notably the Sanpoil and the Shoshone, manufactured a crude type of clay ware, although they were several hundred miles from the nearest deposits of good pottery clay. In basketry, coiling and twining were skillfully employed. Fine decorative effects were achieved with dyes and with a kind of embroidery. In historic times clothing in this area was of the same general character as that of the more easterly peoples. Tanning processes were well understood, as evidenced in the wide use of dressed buckskin, ornamented with fringe; and of skirts, leggings, and moccasins, decorated with beads and porcupine quills. Skin caps and robes were also common.

The culture of the tribes east of the Cascades changed dramatically a few decades before the invasion of the whites. Through the introduction of the horse they had become a more or less nomadic people. The Snakes, Nez Perces, and Cayuses counted their wealth in horses, and because they were thus free to move about they evolved a culture based largely on the chase and warfare. Game and fish, supplemented by roots and berries, was their main source of food.

The culture of Oregon's southeast plateau was of a lower order, owing to the nature of the barren, forbidding country. Rather than discussing all the tribes of this desert country, I shall hereafter refer to them generally as Snake Indians. They were of the Shoshone family. The picture that we get of these Indians—from the accounts of the earliest whites to pass through this country—shows that during the greater part of the year they were scattered over the land in small groups or individual families. They lived on a precarious fare of roots, grasshoppers, crickets, and an occasional jack rabbit or antelope. It was either feast or famine with them. They had no horses and no houses, not even tepees. Their sole protection from the weather was a semicircle of sagebrush to break the wind. Most of the time they went naked or wore a small robe or girdle of rabbit skins. Their few possessions were moved about on the backs of the women. It is likely that at certain times they came together in large groups at some of the lakes to gather roots, or perhaps to fish. They were our poorest and lowest type of Indian in regard to civilization.

In later years, after the immigrants started passing through their country, in the latter forties, they seem to have found it convenient to gather in large bands for protection and to raid the wagon trains passing through. By the time gold was discovered in the John Day country in 1861, they were grouped into quite large bands. They had obtained arms by means of which they caused considerable trouble to the settlers, until they were defeated and rounded up by the soldiers and placed upon reservations.

"Pit Indians"

The Klamath and Modoc culture, influenced by the same factors as the Shoshone but modified by the *tules* (reeds) and *wocas* (yellow water lily) of the Klamath and Tule Lake marshes, presented a definite departure from the culture in other sections of Oregon. The Klamaths and Modocs have been termed "pit Indians" because their dwellings were little more than roofed-over pits sunk about four feet below the surface of the ground. These houses appeared as mounds of earth about six feet high, with a circular hole two and a half feet in diameter at the top, from which a ladder led down into the circular space below. The interior was twenty feet across, with sleeping bunks and arrangements for storing dried meats, seeds, acorns, and roots. The whole was substantially built, the roof being of poles covered with rushes and with earth taken from the pit beneath. On hooks from the rush-lined ceiling hung bags and baskets, laden with such luxuries as dried grasshoppers and berries. About the bunks hung the skins of deer and other smaller game.

The dress of the women consisted of a skirt of deerskin thongs fastened to a braided belt; the men wore breechclouts of deerskin, and the children went entirely naked. When grasshoppers were abundant the Indians scoured the valleys, gathered the insects in great quantities by driving them into pits, and made preparations for a feast. A fire was kindled in one of the pits, and after the latter had been thoroughly heated, the harvest was dropped in, covered with damp *tules* and hot stones, and baked. Prepared in this fashion the insects were eaten with great relish. They were also powdered and mixed with *wocas* meal in a kind of bread baked in the ashes.

Tribal Customs

Among the coastal bands, well-defined classes existed, although there was neither a totemic nor a clan system like that developed among the people of the North. Society was divided into a hereditary nobility, a middle class, and a slave class, composed in the main of captives taken in war and their descendants. A certain degree of economic freedom prevailed; individuals, exclusive of the slaves, were allowed to enjoy most of the fruits of their labors. Social lines, however, were more strictly drawn: marriage between commoners and the wealthier and more important classes was frowned upon to such an extent that disgrace was passed on to the offspring. Government was centered in a chief, whose office as a rule was hereditary, and tribal councils, at which men of importance stated their opinions. Women occupied a position of inferiority, much of the drudgery of daily work falling to their lot. This inferiority was also reflected in the practice of determining descent by the paternal line.

Among the Chinooks, distinctions of rank extended to burial. The bodies of slaves were tossed into the river or gotten rid of in some other way, while the free-born were carefully prepared for box, vault, tree, or canoe burial, and were honored with rituals of mourning which included periods of wailing during a certain length of time, cutting the hair, and refraining from mentioning the name of the dead. Entombment

In olden times, the tribes west of the Cascades often wrapped their dead in robes or mats and deposited them in canoes in the woods or on some rocky point. Occasionally bodies were buried in vaults of cedar boards, or simply placed in trees.

Drawing of canoe burial made by George Gibbs in 1850.

varied according to the tribe and locality. Columbia River Indians utilized Memaloose Island near The Dalles, Mount Coffin near the mouth of the Cowlitz River, and other islands and promontories, with ceremonial dressing and storing of bones. The coast Indians used canoes supported on decorated scaffolds, and placed the head toward the west so that the departed spirit might more easily find its way to *Memaloose Illahee,* or the land of the dead, which lay somewhere toward the setting sun. Valley Indians often placed their dead, wrapped in skins, in the forks of trees.

Compared to the rigid class divisions of the coastal regions, or to the system of the war-hero of the plains area, early social structures east of the Cascades had little class differentiation and were characterized by a general equality and pacifism. Chieftainship was nominally hereditary, but actually depended upon personal qualifications. Holding advisory rather than dictatorial powers, the chief was easily approachable and rarely possessed great individual wealth. Catches of salmon and meat obtained from hunting were divided equally among all present, foreigners included. Slavery, where it did come into existence, was an incident of war rather than an institution.

Chinook Jargon

In prehistoric days, Indian tribes of the Pacific Northwest traded among themselves. They traded skins for meat, roots for fish, arrowheads for canoes, stone implements for skin robes, and slaves for shell money. Hundreds of Indians used to gather at the fishing stations of Wishram and Kettle Falls. Regular pow-wows were held in the Yakima Valley, where the Indians came to trade horses, dance, and gamble. Some of the Columbia Plateau Indians even traveled to Lapwai, Idaho, to attend the "scalp" or "meeting" dance. These Indians needed a common language, and the Chinook Jargon became that language. It became a clearing house for tribal dialects.

The jargon was built up chiefly from words of the Chinook and Nootka tribes, with borrowings from other dialects. With the coming of the trappers, traders, and settlers, words from the

French and English were added. As for the fur traders, an important part of their equipment was their knowledge of the jargon, and ability to use it.

At one time this jargon must have been in daily use by more than a hundred thousand persons. Most of the early settlers of the Pacific Northwest—as well as loggers, miners, and traders—spoke it commonly with the Indians. When the Indians were removed to reservations, many who had not adopted the jargon were obliged to learn it in order to speak with their neighbors. It is permanently recorded in many of the place names of the Northwest, as well as in the history of the trappers and the traders. These are storehouses for its pungent, often poetic, words.

Not until the coming of the railroads and the huge migrations did the jargon fall into disuse. However, some of the words linger, with slight changes in meaning. One still hears an occasional "siwash" (Indian), "skookum" (strong), "potlatch" (celebration), "hi-yu" (plenty), or "wappato" (potato).

Religious Beliefs

All tribes believed in an existence after death, and in a soul that inhabited the body yet was distinct from the vital principle and capable of leaving the body in dreams, faints, and trances—though if it stayed away too long the body died. Other living things were also similarly endowed. So it was that a canoe builder deferentially addressed the tree from which he obtained his log, as though it were a conscious personality, and a fisherman spoke apologetically to the first catch of the season as he took it from the water.

Creation myths varied from tribe to tribe. The creation of men and animals was ascribed by one to *Echanum*, the fire spirit, by some to Coyote, the transformer, who is given credit for creating the tribes from the legs, head, belly, and body of his vanquished enemy, the beaver. Stories of Coyote and Thunderbird were common to many tribes. The Thunderbird was ruler of the storm, avenger, originator of numerous taboos, and creator of volcanic activity. Coyote in a hundred grotesque

31

forms was the hero of many roguish stories, emphasizing his trickery, selfishness, and prurience; and he was the source of rigid taboos regarding foods, domestic economy, and ceremonial observance.

A belief in personal guardian spirits was the most marked characteristic of Indian religious life. These spirits were presumed to bring success in war enterprises and in the acquisition of wealth, rank, and recognition in tribal councils. A boy frequently received a spirit that had been in his family before; a person of high rank was likely to have a powerful spirit, and women or persons of lower classes usually acquired only a small and not very effective guardian spirit. Occasionally, an individual, usually a man, became a *shaman* by acquiring one or more spirits effective in curing illness. These *shamans*, although they could never become chiefs, often rose to great power; and since they could exact high pay for their services, became at times exceedingly rich, even richer than the chief himself.

Concepts of the supernatural, however, varied. The Sanpoils of eastern Washington—who have been carefully studied—divided supernatural beings into five categories: the soul, the soul-spirit, ghosts, spirit-ghosts, and "dangerous beings." During life, they believed, everyone possessed a soul. After death the soul went to the land of the dead at the end of the Milky Way, or stayed on earth and roamed about in the transformed nature of a soul-ghost. Spirits were numerous; plants, animals and inanimate objects were believed to be endowed with spirits, and it was among them that the youth sought his guardian spirit. Once found, a guardian spirit became an integral part of the self, and could not depart without serious physical consequences. Upon the death of the individual, the guardian spirit became a spirit-ghost and might then become the guardian spirit of a relative or of a *shaman*. "Dangerous beings," that is, ogres, monsters, demons, and evil dwarfs, were described in many interesting tales.

Other eastern Washington tribes had their *shamans*, too, with healing and similar supernatural powers bestowed during their quest for their guardian spirits. The *shaman*, who could be either a man or a woman, administered to the sick and officiated at ceremonies. Every winter, for a period of several months, dramatic spirit dances were held in the longhouses as part of initiation ceremonies for novices obtaining a guardian spirit, or as a special occasion under the sponsorship of a prominent *shaman,* or when the guardian spirit of any individual commanded a spirit dance.

Legends were invented by the Indians to explain the origin and form of many geographic features. The story of Loowit, a beautiful Indian girl, who was the subject of a quarrel between rival lovers, and who dwelt on the natural rock Bridge of the Gods which once spanned the Columbia River at the Cascades, tells of the destruction of the bridge and the creation of the three great mountain peaks — Mount St. Helens, Mount Adams, and Mount Hood. Another legend has it that Neahkahnie Mountain on the coast reached its present form from a single blow of the hatchet of Coyote, who built a fire on the mountainside, heated rocks and threw them into the sea, where the seething waters grew into waves that have been crashing against the shore ever since. Mitchell Point, once called the "Storm King" by the Indians, was believed by them to have been built to part the storm clouds that hurried up the Columbia.

Although Northwest Indians have abandoned most of their tribal ways, at times drums still throb above the music and words of tribal songs, and busy feet pattern the ceremonial dances. There are the annual root festivals of the Warm Springs tribes and the Umatillas; the huckleberry feasts of the Yakimas and Klamaths; the sun dances at Fort Hall; and at Soap Lake, Washington, Northwest tribes assemble annually for rituals and dances. The salmon feast on the Columbia is still generally held, and there are a number of other gatherings for rodeos, carnivals, and other celebrations, many of fairly recent origin.

A festival common throughout the coastal regions north of the Columbia, but especially important in the Puget Sound country, was the potlatch, a ceremonial feast at which valuable gifts were distributed to friends and neighboring tribesmen, each of whom was obligated to respond in a similar manner at a potlatch of his own. These feasts are still observed in a modified form. In the coastal areas, too, secret societies reached moderate development. Among modern festivals are Treaty Days celebrated in some reservations with a period of feasting, water sports, dances, songs, games, and exhibits of native handiwork. One of the most interesting of these celebrations is held annually in August on Whidbey Island, at which Puget Sound bands engage in war canoe races and other water sports.

The Lower Columbia

The bulk of Indian relics comes from the river banks, lakes, and some small streams. Along the banks of the lower Columbia there is not a bar that the Indians have not lived or camped upon. There was always a reason for the location of a house or even a tepee village. Food supply and transportation were the controlling factors. Water was always at hand from the river. Fuel could be reached in the forest. Shade trees, beautiful scenery, or the like—that would influence a white man—were remote to the mind of an Indian. Practical things only were considered.

Because their food supply was nearby, Indians of the lower Columbia had rather permanent habitations. The first white men found them living in wood houses occupied by several families. It would appear that a friendly group of families, perhaps related, got together and built the big house. About it, close by, or strung along the bank, might be found several or many houses of individual families or groups. It appeared that these houses were used as long as repairs would keep them standing, with little or no regard for parasitic dwellers. This long occupancy by many people enriched the sandy soil about the houses with relics. It also encouraged the making of heavier pieces such as large mortars, as they did not need to be moved. There are no remains of these houses other than the pits, some indications of which are occasionally found. There was a record-breaking flood in the Willamette River in 1861 and one in the Columbia River in 1894. Many wooden relics were carried away by the water.

Sites of long-occupied houses and villages can be determined by the number, the kinds, and the depths of the relics, and from the depth or thickness of the camp dirt. By "camp dirt" I mean that where a site has been used a long time—for generations or perhaps ages—the refuse of the camp will stain or discolor the natural yellowish or brownish silt to a deep black, and to a depth of from one to four feet. Under examination, this dirt will be found to be full of fine particles of shell, bone, chippings, ashes, and the like. Naturally such places make good digging ground for relics.

Sometimes camp sites with deep camp dirt are found located back from the main river on sloughs not connected with the present stream. The reason for this was likely a change in the river channel which cut the Indians off from the open river; they would then move their village. Many sites have been carried away as river currents cut into the banks. Other sites have been buried by the sand deposits of high floods. I have not found much camp dirt along the river east of the mountains, probably because of the way the sand bars blow in and out, and the forever drifting sands.

The wonderful canoes of these lower river Indians were once plentiful; now they are all gone. The old canoe-makers are also gone, and the young folks are taking to power boats. Fortunately, museums have preserved a few of these fine large canoes. The later canoes were made with the white men's tools, though they were modeled from primitive ones.

Years of hunting and studying Indian relics have led to some interesting thoughts, one of the most intriguing being—how did the relics happen to be in the positions in which I occasionally found them on the river bars? In some places, they were scattered from the surface to the bottom. Occasionally they were only at the top, and again only near the bottom. Let us start from the beginning:

An Indian group moves onto a sand bar never previously occupied. They bring with them their different implements, and they continually make more of them. They do not have bureau

35

drawers, cupboards, or attics for keeping things. Their belongings may be put around the walls in their houses, or just left carelessly about. There are many children and also dogs. A youngster may pick up an article, carry it away some distance in play, and of course never bring it back. There is much refuse about. A dog scratching in this refuse covers the implement. Perhaps the article lies on the surface until a mole probes up dirt and covers it. A woman may drive a stake into the ground to make a drying rack. When she takes the rack down, she doesn't fill the stake hole. The children, or the woman herself, may kick an article into the hole. It is on its way. The group go to the mountains to pick berries. They don't trust the other Indians who pass to and fro on the river. They bury their heavier pieces. They meet with misfortune, sickness, or an enemy tribe. They don't come back. . .Or, a tribe may be caught by an unusually high flood. They rush their things into canoes and make for high ground, abandoning many articles in the rush. When the flood passes, it leaves several inches of sandy sediment over the camp site. It is the tendency of a stone article in the ground to go downward, not upward, and there are many means by which it can be helped on its way. . .Given sufficient time, many things can happen to enrich a camp site with almost any and every kind of artifact.

The principal foods of these lower Columbia River Indians were the wappato and the camas, among the plant world; and waterfowl, deer, and salmon from the animal world. These were varied by the use of many other kinds of plants and roots, some of which were used only as seasoning.

Of all the plants used by the Indians, not only on the Columbia but by western Indians generally, the most important and widely known was the camas. There is more romance and adventure clustered about the camas root and flower than about almost any other American plant. Hardly one of the early Pacific explorers but records how at some time the camas has saved him from extreme hunger, if not from actual starvation. In the traditions of the Indians it was given a prominent place; many mythical tales are told of its origin and uses.

INDIAN PLANT FOODS

Upper left: Wappato—its bulbs resemble Irish potatoes but have a sweetish taste, much like chestnuts. *Upper right:* Camas—primitive cooks used its bulb for bread. *Bottom:* Wocas—Indians ground the seeds of this pond lily and made excellent flour.

Camas fields were tribal property, jealously guarded against trespass. Wars were sometimes caused by disputes over questions of possession or boundary, nor could the Indians understand why the white man was privileged to usurp these possessions and destroy the camas meadows with his plow. The Nez Perce War, under the able leadership of Chief Joseph, was a final desperate protest against these trespasses upon their fields. The modern Nez Perces eat their camas with sugar and cream, luxuries of which their forefathers, of course, knew nothing.

Relics have often been found in the camas and other root fields and meadows, where they were carried for use in digging. In the lower river country these places were close at hand.

It is rather interesting to know that the places the hunters and collectors have found the richest in relics have been the sites occupied as villages when the whites first came. I have been personally interested in examining the sites mentioned as villages by Lewis and Clark, and have found them to be the finest spots along the river. Does this mean a shorter occupancy of this territory by Indians than we are accustomed to believe, or is it just that these larger villages had been on this same spot for the last hundred years or so, and the floods had destroyed the older sites? Can we expect that there may be larger and richer old sites back from the present channel, and buried under several feet of deposited sand? I think this might be so as we all know what the river can do. On slough bottoms during surveying I have dug for iron pipes that the records show were set as property corners over forty years ago, and have found them covered two to four feet with sand and sediment. In some places I have seen pioneer fence posts projecting only a foot above the ground level.

The Upper Columbia

When I refer to the upper river, or the upper Columbia, I mean that section of the Columbia beginning at an indefinite point between Hood River and The Dalles and extending upstream to the mouth of the Snake River. There is no division of tribes at these boundaries, but there is a main division within them. On the north bank the old village of Wishram was the farthest east of the Chinooks. The old Indians called it "Wishum." (The Indian town of Wishram is downstream about ten miles from the railroad town of Wishram.) Above this village the language changed. On the south bank, the Chinooks extended a few miles farther east.

These Indians experienced the same physical changes caused by the Cascades as the Indians to the north and south of them. The mountains cut off the rainfall that comes from the coast. About Hood River the Douglas fir begins to disappear, and there is the appearance of oak and pine. These fade out at The Dalles, leaving barren hills covered with sagebrush. Occasionally bunches of willows are found along the river banks, and a few juniper trees can be seen on the highest benches of the cliffs. It is colder here in winter and hotter in the summer than it is west of the Cascades.

The Indians in this upper river country still depended on salmon, but they often had to travel considerable distances for other means of livelihood. Because of the open country and the excellent pasturage, they could use horses, but they still had many canoes. The river banks were not desirable places in which to live because of the disagreeable winds and the drifting sands. Hence many families had their homes back on interior streams and came to the river only in the salmon season. They also had greater distances to go to reach their good hunting grounds and berry patches. This traveling about over a large territory caused a wider distribution of their relics.

I consider the heavy stone work of these upper Columbia Indians somewhat inferior to that of the lower river Indians, but this might have been because their village sites were not so permanent. Their chipped artifacts, however, are of the very best. Dealers and collectors quite generally consider the arrowheads of this territory to be the finest in the world. The selection of beautiful material, the use of artistic shapes, and the delicate workmanship all combine to make these beautiful points. The fact that these Indians were far more warlike than those of the lower river might, in a measure, account for their fine arrow points. The very best points were war arrows, and these are the ones appearing most often as grave offerings.

It is puzzling to note the comparatively small use of obsidian along the Columbia River. This material was within their reach and was highly prized by all the interior tribes, yet only about ten per cent of the river artifacts are made of it. The other ninety per cent are of agate, chalcedony, jasper, agatized wood, common opal, and other pretty stone—some of which came from the gravel bars along the river.

For ages the sand has been drifting, covering and uncovering the relics. Even in my own time I have known bars to be blown out to bedrock and then blown back again. These changes during the ages have enriched the ground along the banks from top to bottom. Today objects are continually coming to light as bars are gradually cut away. Some of these have not been blown out since the Indian days. There are many large bars that have been only slightly wind-cut since the coming of the whites; and these are, without doubt, full of relics that may yet come to light.

As the ground on these camp sites is nearly barren of plant life, the blown-out relics lie in plain sight; and the hunting is easy and pleasant; just keep moving and keep your eyes on the ground watching for signs. As in any other game, knowledge and experience help.

Low or wash gravel bars have been enriched when nearby camp sites have disintegrated. These are much easier to work than those of the lower river. The filling between the gravel is sand, while on the lower river it is clay. Agate hunters will also find that these upper river sites are interesting, and so will the relic hunters, because the sites are strewn with the beautiful pieces of stone from which the Indians were in the process of making chipped implements.

In past years the hunting of relics in this upper river country was quite ideal. It is now more picked over, of course, and the great dams have drowned some of the finest places, like the Long Narrows, formerly a five-mile stretch of turbulent water above The Dalles. Many likely spots, though, remain; but nowadays more relics can often be obtained by digging than by surface hunting.

If you are hunting this upper-river country, be prepared for a sand storm. Frequently, I have fought these storms until my ears and hair became filled with sand. I have tried seeking relief or a rest behind large boulders or points of cliffs, but they are no good. They make an eddy that is as disagreeable to face as the storm. It is best to take to the willows along the bank, if you can find any. These seem to break the wind and to screen out most of the sand. . .Still, a quiet summer evening on the upper Columbia River is among nature's wonders.

Indians Fishing at old Celilo Falls on the Columbia River.

Part Two

INDIAN CAMP SITES AND VILLAGES

THE PLACES WHERE HUNTERS AND COLLECTORS HAVE SECURED the most relics have been those occupied as villages when the whites first came. Among the larger Columbia River sites mentioned by early whites was the Chinook village on the Washington shore near the mouth of the river. Though now washed away, it was at one time the headquarters of Chief Concomly, the principal chief of the confederacy of all the Chinook tribes along the Columbia between the Cascade Range and the sea, except for the Clatsops. On the south bank of the river, Chief Cobaway ruled independently. His lodge was where Fort Stevens was located, and his people ranged the plains between present Astoria and Gearhart.

For well over a century the most famous relic from the Chinook site, the old chief's skull, rested in a British museum near Portsmouth, far from the river waters and the land where Concomly lived, ruled, and died. In 1835, five years after his death, a young Scots surgeon stationed at Fort Vancouver exhumed the head—in the questionable interest of science—and made off with it. The only blood shed at the decapitation was the young doctor's, who suffered a severe hemorrhage from the physical exertion. In 1953 the skull was returned and now has a place of honor in the Flavel Museum at Astoria, where Concomly's rival Chief Cobaway once ruled.

Old Cathlamet, near Tongue Point on the south shore, is another site mentioned by the explorers, but it is also washed away. At the time it was first visited by the explorers, though, it had some three to four hundred inhabitants who prospered till the fatal fever of the early 1830s decimated their numbers.

This epidemic, sometimes called intermittent fever, took the lives of from one half to three fourths of the Indian population of the entire Northwest. Survivors of the Cathlamet village later moved across the river and settled near the present Cathlamet, Washington.

One of the sights that Lewis and Clark noted among the Cathlamets was their strange burial custom. The dead Indian was placed in one of their beautiful canoes which in turn was placed high in some cottonwood or balm-of-Gilead tree, with the sharp prow pointed westward. With all his worldly wealth of furs and trinkets placed about him and with every paddle in position, he awaited new life. Forty miles away could be heard the moaning of the Columbia Bar—and the ocean winds swayed the branches of his aerial grave.

At Astoria in 1961, in commemoration of the town's 150th anniversary, a replica of an Indian burial canoe was placed atop 650-foot Coxcomb Hill. Following Indian tradition, the canoe points westward to the Pacific Ocean, the home of Father Salmon who provided the natives with their main source of food.

To sacrifice a canoe was to make a great gift. These canoes were the work of years. They were hollowed out with fire and stone and with beaver-tooth chisels; they were steamed with red-hot rocks and water, and were stretched to just the right size and shape, and held in place with stretchers painstakingly sewed in. They were beautiful, practical, and swift. And they were safe, save for one weakness: where the cedar was hewn across the grain to form the lines for the stern and bow; in a heavy sea this area would always work, sometimes splitting the canoe from end to end. The older Indians told of clutching onto the sides of a split canoe for hours and sometimes days, until they were rolled ashore by the surf.

Sauvies Island

Of all camp sites along the lower river, perhaps the most famous are on Sauvies Island, at the junction of the Columbia and Willamette rivers. Island Indians were in a way protected;

individual families lived along the river banks both above and below, acting—no doubt unconsciously—as sentinels. Yet this was not the primary cause of the large population or long occupancy of the island. Food supply, transportation, and the meeting of two large rivers were the controlling factors.

Sauvies Island is about sixteen miles long and some five miles across at its widest. In Indian times it was open woodland dotted with many lakes; now it is diked and occupied by many fine farms. For relic hunters the site of the Reeder Land Claim, on the location of old Multnomah village, has produced more finds than any other special location on the island. However, it was merely one of dozens of sites long occupied as villages, particularly on the upstream half of the island. The shores opposite the island in both directions, especially the Columbia bank from Lewis River to opposite the upper end of the island, are spotted with camp sites and have produced many relics. The best hunting there now is in plowed fields or where floods have washed the bank away.

This was the setting for much of Frederic Homer Balch's Indian romance, *The Bridge of the Gods.* He wrote (1891): "The chiefs of the Willamettes gathered on Wappato Island, from time immemorial the council-ground of the tribes. The white man has changed its name to Sauvies Island; but its wonderful beauty is unchangeable. Lying at the mouth of the Willamette River and extending many miles down the Columbia, rich in wide meadows and crystal lakes, its interior dotted with majestic oaks and its shores fringed with cottonwoods, around it the blue and sweeping rivers, the wooded hills, and the far white snow peaks—it is the most picturesque spot in Oregon."

As far as known, the first white men to visit Sauvies Island were Lieutenant William Broughton from Captain George Vancouver's exploring expedition, in October 1792, and Lewis and Clark in November 1805. Young Broughton left the armed tender *Chatham* in the lower river and proceeded upstream in the cutter and launch with twenty-five men and some friendly Indians, to become the first whites to ascend and explore the river for a hundred miles. At the lower end of Sauvies Island they saw twenty-three Indian canoes with about 150 Indians drawn up in warlike formation. Sending gifts ahead to show friendly intentions, Broughton was allowed to proceed. For obvious reasons, he named the location where he saw the canoes Warrior Point, a name it has retained.

They continued (October 28) "up the main branch of the river until eight in the evening; when, under the shelter of some willows, they took up their lodging for the night on a low sandy point." This is now called Willow Bar Point and is on the east side of the island. Arriving at the upper end of the island, where the main channel of the Willamette flows into the Columbia, they named this Belle Vue Point because of the magnificent view of a lofty snow-covered mountain—which Broughton named Hood in honor of Lord Samuel Hood, a member of the British Board of Admiralty.

Of the Indians here, the young lieutenant reported: "The natives differed in nothing very materially from those we had visited during the summer (at Nootka), but in the decoration of their persons; in this respect, they surpassed all the other tribes with paints of different colours, feathers, and other ornaments." And the Indians lived well in this land of the camas and wappato: "The skirts (edges) of the woods afforded a most excellent green vegetable, resembling in appearance and taste the turnip-top when young. A bulbous root, about the size, and not unlike the crocus, that ate much like mealy potato, wild mint, ground ivy, and wild lavender, all these the natives make great use of, together with berries of various kinds, particularly the cranberry, of a most excellent flavor, and the first we had seen on this coast."

Thirteen years later, on November 4, 1805, Captains Meriwether Lewis and William Clark, with their crew of thirty, reached this part of the lower Columbia, after a trip of some four thousand miles. They were not enthusiastic about their reception. Of their journey downstream, while approaching and passing Sauvies Island, Clark wrote:

"A number of Indians. . .came down for the purpose as we supposed of paying us a friendly visit as they had put on their favorite dresses. In addition to their usual covering they had scarlet and blue blankets, sailor's jackets and trousers and skirts and hats. They had, all of them, as well as their war axes, spears and bows and arrows, or muskets and pistols with tin powder flasks. We smoked with them and endeavored to show them every attention but we soon found them very assuming and disagreeable companions. While we were eating they stole the pipe with which they were smoking and the great coat of one of the men.

"We immediately searched them all and discovered the coat stuffed under the root of a tree near where they were sitting, but the pipe we could not recover. Finding us determined with them, they showed their displeasure in the only way which they dared by returning in an ill humor to their village. We then proceeded and soon met two canoes with 12 men who were on their way from below. The larger of the canoes was ornamented with a figure of a bear in the bow and a man in the stern, both made of painted wood and very neatly fixed to the boat. In the same canoe were two Indians finely dressed with round hats.

"These circumstances induced us to give the name of Image-Canoe to the large island (a group of islands including Hayden), the lower end of which we now passed at the distance of nine miles from its head . . . The river was now about a mile and a half in width with a gentle current; three miles below Image-Canoe Island we came to four large houses on the left side (Sauvies Island side). A mile lower we passed a single house on the left and another on the right. We continued on until we then landed at a distance of seven miles below after night, in hopes of getting rid of the Indians who now followed us and were very troublesome."

Had Captain Clark had access to Broughton's account, he might have been more sympathetic with the Indians' delight at the American pipe and tobacco. In his October 1792 report to George Vancouver, covering his excursion into this vicinity, Broughton had observed: "The inhabitants are universally addicted to smoking. Their pipe is similar to ours in shape; the bowl is made of very hard wood, and is externally ornamented with carvings; the tube, about two feet long, is made of a small branch of the elder. In this they smoke an herb, which the country produces, of a very mild nature; and by no means unpleasant; they however took great pleasure in smoking our tobacco; hence it is natural to conclude, it might become a valuable article of traffic amongst them. . ." (Journals of the trappers and fur traders confirm the importance of tobacco as a valuable trade goods.)

Indian Tobacco

Because smoking was largely a matter of ceremony and religion, the Indians often decorated their pipes extensively, and these have been found in a wide variety of materials including clay, stone, wood, and bone. The stone pipes have withstood the elements best, and many more of them have been found than those of other materials. A native tobacco (*Nicotiana quadrivalvis*) was the only plant cultivated by the western Indians, and its culture was of a very primitive form. It consisted merely of scattering the seeds of this rank weed in the ashes of a tract of ground that had been burned over, and then allowing the plants to grow with no further care. Indians of the coast tribes added the lime from burned shells to the tobacco leaves to temper their harshness.

This tobacco grew wild along the western streams and is variously referred to as wild tobacco, Indian tobacco, and native tobacco. The entire plant is sticky-hairy. It has a stout, branching stem and grows from one to two feet high. It has a few white flowers and is characterized by a rather unpleasant scent. In his *Journal* for 1824-1826, David Douglas, the botanist, reported his experience with the plant:

"I first saw a single plant of it in the hand of an Indian at the Great Falls of the Columbia, but though I offered two ounces of manufactured tobacco, an enormous remuneration, he would on no account part with it. The *Nicotiana* is never sowed by the Indians near the villages lest it should be pulled and

Morton Collection

Columbia River tube pipes.

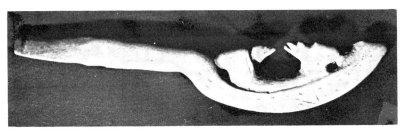

Reeder Collection

Bone artifact of unknown use, found on Sauvies Island.

used before it comes to perfect maturity; they select for its cultivation an open place in the wood, where they burn a dead tree or stump, and strewing the ashes over the ground, plant the tobacco there. Fortunately, I happened to detect one of these little plantations, and supplied myself, without delay or immediate stipulations for payment, with both specimens for drying and seeds. The owner, whom I shortly met, seeing the prize under my arm, appeared much displeased, but was propitiated with a present of European tobacco, and becoming good friends with me, gave the above description of its culture, saying that wood ashes invariably made it grow very large."

During the night following the theft of the pipe by the Indians, the Lewis and Clark expedition had more trouble. The following day, November 5, Clark recorded: "Our choice of a camp had been very unfortunate; for on a sand island opposite to us there were immense numbers of geese, swan, ducks and other wild fowl which during the whole night serenaded us with a confusion of noises which prevented our sleeping. We left camp at an early hour and after passing villages on both sides of the river and traveling eight or ten miles, we observed behind a sharp bend of rocks (Warrior Point on Sauvies Island) a channel a quarter of a mile wide (Multnomah Channel of the Willamette) which we supposed must be the one used by Indians yesterday on leaving Image-Canoe Island."

The fever which raged throughout the Northwest in the early 1830s destroyed nearly the whole island population. Dr. John McLoughlin removed the few survivors to the mainland at Fort Vancouver. In 1834, Captain Nathaniel J. Wyeth built a trading post on the island and named the post Fort William. He wrote: "This Wappato Island which I have selected for our establishment, consists of woodland and prairie and on it there is considerable deer and those who could spare time to hunt might live well but mortality has carried off to a man its inhabitants and there is nothing to attest that they ever existed except their decaying houses, their graves and their unburied bones of which there are heaps."

Wappato patch, Sauvies Island.

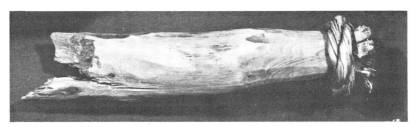

Wood wedge from Sauvies Island.

Because of opposition from the Hudson's Bay Company, Wyeth abandoned his project in 1836 and five years later McLoughlin established a dairy on the island, placing Laurent Sauve, a retired trapper, in charge. The island takes its name from this old Hudson's Bay trapper-dairyman.

Some five to ten years later, when the settlers moved in on the island, the brush that had grown over the old village sites was still scattered full of bones and relics. Nothing had been taken away. The upstream half of the island is higher above water, and hence not so subject to the June freshets. The sites on the lower half show less occupancy, as the Indians knew they must move every early summer and perhaps sometimes in the winter. The lower part, though, was ideal country in late summer. Camas and wappato were very plentiful, and young ducks were in every pond.

There are several interesting camp sites showing quite large areas of black dirt in the interior of the island. There are also, in the interior of the island, signs of sloughs, now filled or nearly so, that must have been open in the Indians' day. These sloughs would have given them "canoe connections" with their outside world.

I have found much pleasant hunting on the Oregon side of the island. Both it and the mainland still contain plenty of relics in the ground. A village site on the Henrici Donation Land Claim has caved into the river, taking an old road and several rows of apple trees. A Captain Sheldon made a fine collection from this site during the eighties and nineties. In idle times the Captain tied his tugboat there and hunted.

Along the lake banks and sloughs quite often one comes upon a gravel bar. Examination will show that the gravel is just on the surface; it is really all Indian rocks. During the course of long years of occupancy of one site, Indians carried in so many rocks that when the floods of later days dissolved the site, there was enough gravel to make the place look like any river gravel bar. Because there is so much sediment in this soil, these gravel bars are hard to comb, but they have produced some fine specimens, and there may still be many small sites on the island that have not yet been uncovered. These will likely be found when the heavy growth of ash and cottonwood is cleared from the ridges along some of the sloughs.

An experienced hunter, who knew the island, used to be able in a day's hunt to pick up from half a dozen to two dozen good chipped specimens and occasionally a good stone piece.

The island has, in the past years, produced an immense supply of relics of all kinds common to these lower river Indians; and will, for years to come, slowly produce more, as plenty are left underground. While many fine pieces of chipped rock have been found, showing that some of these Indians were capable of fine workmanship, the average of their work is not equal to that found on the upper river. Whether or not this was caused by lack of necessity in obtaining a livelihood or just lack of skill, I can't say. A great number of very small arrowheads, from one-fourth to three-fourths inch long, are found here. This is natural because the island once teemed with waterfowl at all seasons.

Though their chipped rock work was not of the best, they did excel in stone work. The island has produced many large ornamental bowls and stone images.

Robert Bonser, for many years county surveyor of Multnomah County, told of the fate of one of these stone images. When he was a young man living on Sauvies Island, an Englishman was farming a place there. In the field was a large stone image. The Englishman plowed around it for a couple of seasons; then, getting tired of the nuisance of it, he made a sled, rolled the image onto it, hauled it to the Willamette Slough, and rolled it over the bank. It is likely still there. This was close to the county line between Multnomah and Columbia counties.

Siwash Wappato

Wappato is a Chinook jargon word of Indian origin and has a variety of spellings, the favored seeming to be *wappato*. It refers to the tasty tuberous root of *Sagittaria latifolia*. After the Irish potato was introduced by the whites, it became the wappato and the other the *siwash wappato*. Fittingly, a small potato-shipping town in Washington's Yakima Valley is named Wapato.

Leslie Haskin chose the wappato for the opening page of his *Wild Flowers of the Pacific Coast.* "This, the first flower of our book, is unalterably linked with first things in the history of the Columbia River Valley, and the old Northwest. Long before the white man visited this coast it was one of the most important plant foods of the natives, especially of the Chinooks of the Lower Columbia, and was an article of well organized commerce between them and the surrounding tribes . . . the plant is woven into their age-old stories as being an article of food in the mythical times 'Before the salmon came to the Columbia.'

"The edible part of the plant is the smooth, solid tuber growing in the soft mud at the bottom of the pond. It is not possible to secure these tubers by pulling the plant, as they are borne at the extremity of long, flabby, root-stocks, and are sure to break off and be lost if disturbed. To secure them the squaws entered the water, often nearly shoulder-deep, and, supporting themselves by clinging to small canoes, rooted them out with their toes. When the bulb was dislodged it immediately rose to the surface, and was then tossed into the canoe. Boiled, they are very good, and resemble Irish potatoes, though with a sweetish flavor suggesting chestnuts. A genuine Indian feast, such as I was recently privileged to enjoy, consisting of wappato and bear's meat, is not to be despised. From the *Journals* of Lewis and Clark it appears that their principal diet during their winter in Oregon was elk beef, secured by their hunters, and wappato bulbs purchased from the Indians."

The wappato is a handsome plant with arrow-shaped leaves; because of these leaves another common name for it is arrowhead. It raises spikes of waxy-white flowers above the water "along the shores of quiet lakes and sluggish streams," preferring the shallows, where the water is from a few inches to several feet deep; but it will grow wherever the soil is always muddy. Sauvies Island was an ideal spot.

Around Portland

Chinook Indians were the first to use the site of Portland as a port. They found it an ideal spot for tieing up their canoes on trading trips between the Columbia and Willamette rivers; and they cleared about an acre of ground gathering wood for their campfires. The first white travelers found a large wood Indian house of many families just below present St. Johns in north Portland. Exactly when the house disappeared is not known. A very high flood in 1861 would certainly have floated any wood from the ground. In pioneer times, Portland boys hunted arrowheads here; it was then spoken of as "The Mouth of Gatton's Slough." Over the years the location produced a considerable amount of both stone and chipped pieces, but now it is filled over for industrial use.

Members of the Oregon Archaeological Society excavating an ancient village site near Scappoose. The site is dug in five-foot squares, one foot level at a time, and all artifacts are recorded in the position found.

A number of "finds" in the St. Johns area have resulted from excavation work at Simmons Road, to drain swampland into the Columbia River slough, in preparation for construction of a lime plant. This was the site of an Indian campground or village; arrowheads, knives and various tools have been found there in considerable quantity. The tools are mostly carved from the bones of some animal. The smaller arrowheads, ranging from a half inch to an inch in size, are usually agate and are variously colored.

Lewis and Clark noted a village of twenty-three mat houses on the Oregon shore of the Columbia opposite the lower end of Government Island, which is almost within the city limits of Portland. I was told by an old pioneer, who had lived on the bank there in the early days, that the camp site had gone into the river a long time ago, and also that the section had been left covered with over a foot of silt by a flood in 1876. All I ever found there was a poor pestle which was sticking out of the bank about two feet from the top.

Mouth of the Clackamas

Old sites that have been filled over for industrial use include the areas occupied by the Portland Airport, the Portland Gas and Coke Company, the Oregon Shipyards, and the Vancouver Shipyards across the river. Another of these sites is on the ground between Guilds Lake and the Willamette River, about two miles above and on the opposite bank of the river from Gatton's Slough. The North Pacific Lumber Company mill stood on this site for about twenty years and finally burned. While surveying the ground a number of years ago, I picked up a couple of banded sinkers there that had been thrown out when pier holes were being dug for the mill.

The mouth of the Clackamas River must have been a good fishing place because the land about it has produced many specimens. Pieces can still be picked up along the banks of the river, but the concentration always appears at the good fishing spots.

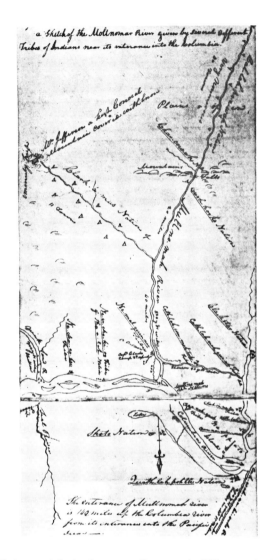

Lewis and Clark map of the Portland area. Shown are the Willamette (top), Clackamas (top left), Columbia, Sandy (bottom left) rivers, and Vancouver Lake (bottom
center); Sauvies Island (bottom right), and thirteen Indian villages.

Abandoned dugout canoe.

The Indians knew their salmon and they had many ways of taking them. Some of our modern methods were learned from them. The fish wheels of the Columbia were suggested by the dipping nets of the Indians. There were two kinds of dip nets used on the rivers. One was a round net on a long handle, which was used from the banks or a platform built out over the rapids. The other was an oblong net, which was used from a canoe drifting down with the current.

Willamette Falls

For many centuries the Indians at Willamette Falls speared salmon and other fish from along the river's rocky banks and ledges. During the seasonal salmon runs there were considerable gatherings here. Though some Indians were in permanent residence, others came from miles around. Pioneers report that many collections of relics have been made here; and it is not unusual to see mortars in the yards of the older residents.

For well over a century, Oregon City has occupied the principal village sites near the falls. Arrow points and an occasional carved rock are still sometimes brought to light during construction work about the town, and the river banks still turn out a few relics in times of flood. There is some grave robbing of rather modern graves along the west bank, producing almost nothing but trade beads.

I do not mean to give the impression that the few sites I have spoken of produced all the relics found in this section of the country. It is apparent, however, that the bars where the first whites found Indian villages were the richest places. There were not many rich spots found other than these. There was a reason for the location of a village; perhaps that reason had existed since the arrival of the first Indians, and possibly no change in their habits took place unless floods caused a material change in the topography.

Indian camps would move as the river banks changed, and this was ordinarily a gradual process. The white man has brought about much more rapid change with his dams and his construction work. Since the Willamette River is smaller than the Columbia, it is not so subject to wave action or winds; hence it remains more stationary.

Fishers Landing

Fishers Landing on the north bank of the Columbia above Vancouver is good "Indian ground." There are some very interesting carvings on flat ground here, and many relics have come from the river bars. Here and at many other places along the Columbia you can find boulders or low cliffs that are spotted with few or many pits. The pits are cone shaped and range between one and four inches in diameter. I have heard it claimed that these pits were made by Indians who were in the process of roughing up the ends of their fire-making sticks. I think there are too many of them to explain them thus.

In the training of boys, many tasks were used. If making these pits was one of them, it could account for the large numbers on the same rock and for the different depths and sizes, as well as for the quite noticeably different ages of the pits.

These pitted boulders are found in other parts of the world besides Oregon. They have been found along some South American rivers, where duckbill scrapers, similar to those of the Columbia, have also been discovered. It is not improbable that the

Pitted boulder at Fishers Landing.

This carved rock found at Fishers has 30 ribs, weighs 200 pounds, and measures 17x19 inches

boulders served much the same purpose there. I have found them only in Chinookan territory along the rivers; I have seen a number of them on the cliffs at Wishram.

Rock Mounds

Many small mounds are found scattered about the foothills of the Cascade Mountains, on the low benches, and in spots where the debris is made up of stones which are rather heavy for one person to lift. These mounds are roughly six feet long, three feet wide at the base, and two feet high at the center. You may find an isolated one, or, in some places, a dozen or more. They have puzzled many people; and some, thinking the mounds were graves, have sweated through an hour or so of good hard work, throwing the stones aside to dig for relics. They got what was coming to them—nothing. Others have thought the mounds were fortifications and have visioned a lively battle there.

The most probable reason for the mounds is that, like the boulder pits, they were made by young men performing a task given them by their counselors in the course of training. The purpose of the task would have been to give them strength and to teach them to obey and have respect for their elders.

Washougal

Along the north bank of the Columbia, in the vicinity of Washougal, there are the remains of many villages. In one place there are nine house pits in a row. The stone work and chipping in this area are very good. One interesting artifact is found from here to Skamania in large numbers, yet it is very scarce in other places. It is a type of knife that some call the "broad horn" or "mule ear."

The river banks here show many fire lines. By these, I mean dark horizontal streaks that may be at various levels in the cutting banks. They show where there was once a surface. In some places the discoloration is slight. This is because only a light vegetable growth has had time to decay and form enough soil.

Heavy growth causes a heavy marking. Thus in some places, on other levels, the marking may be very prominent. Examination may show charcoal, ashes, flint chippings, and other remains of the Indian life during the time that level was surface. These fire lines make an interesting study.

After every flood a few relics can be found that come from these cutting banks. Many trade beads have been taken from this section of the river, but I am sorry to say that most of them came from graves—many of which are not even old.

Here is a relic story of the Washougal country that you may believe as much of as you like; I can vouch for only my part of it: Lewis and Clark records show that they gave out three large-size medals in Oregon. One of these, I believe, is held by someone in the Pendleton or La Grande country, one is in the possession of the Oregon Historical Society, and the third has never come to light. Many years ago, a friend, who is a member of a pioneer family of the Washougal country, remarked that he was on the trail of "something you will like for your collection." He then said that there was an old Indian living up there with whom he was quite friendly. This Indian had told him that when his grandfather died they had buried with him a round medal which the first white people to come down the river had given his grandfather, who was an important chief. Then my friend said,

"I'll bet I find out, before the winter is over, where that old Indian is buried." About a year later, I again met this friend and asked what success he had had with the old Indian. His answer was,

"He died suddenly, just when I was getting along fine with him; and he had promised to show me that old burial place."

The area between Washougal and Skamania was sparsely occupied because of the poor hunting and lack of vegetation. Here is the famous Columbia Gorge, where the river has gouged a route through the Cascade Mountains. At Skamania begins a populous area because here were the cascades of the river, providing ideal fishing grounds.

"Big Mouth" Sites

Memory fails as to whether these Indians were called the "Big Mouth" or "Big Nose" tribe. However, the sites I mean began at the town of Skamania on the Washington side of the Columbia and extended upstream to about Beacon Rock, which was a landmark for river voyagers for more than a century. Now it is surmounted by a beacon to guide airplanes. Lewis and Clark noted villages here; and I once had occasion to be on this ground for about a month.

At that time relics were very plentiful, though the people living nearby said almost all of them had been picked up. They said it used to be that one could walk along the beach and discover a few arrowheads at any time. One day I found four pretty fair mortars within fifty feet of each other, and banded net-sinkers were everywhere along the water's edge. These were more plentiful along that part of the river than farther downstream, perhaps because the swifter current required the use of more sinkers—or, again, it may be that the large eddy in the river here was an unusually good fishing place. These sinkers and other stone pieces can still be picked up on the gravel bars which the floods keep turning over.

The sites are now practically all washed away.

I found a rather interesting relic while hunting just below the mouth of Woodward Creek. I was carelessly raking down the face of an eight-foot sand bank that was cutting away when my army grubhoe struck something hard. After I had dug in a little way, a four-pound cannon ball rolled out. It was coated with rust that came off in pieces like the peeling of an orange. The story goes that, during the Indian wars of 1855-56, a boatload of soldiers was being taken up the river to the relief of the Cascades. A cannon was set up on deck and when a group of Indians was seen on the bank, a shot was taken at them. The Oregon Historical Society has a twin to this ball that was found about three miles farther upstream. It is said to have been found in a large rotten stump. My cannon ball was about six feet below the surface. How far it had penetrated I could not tell.

Upriver from Beacon Rock is Bonneville Dam, which impounds the river water up to The Dalles Dam. It is named for Captain Benjamine de Bonneville, whose western exploits were set forth in *The Adventures of Captain Bonneville,* by Washington Irving, well over a hundred years ago.

Many Indian camp sites and villages were submerged by this impoundment of the water, including the Cascades rapids and the old shore line. Bradford Island, an ancient Indian burial ground, separates the river's two channels at the site of the dam.

The Cascades

In the area of the Cascades in the Columbia Gorge there began a series of rapids and whirlpools and a complete change of environment for the Indians. Westward it was mostly impenetrable forest and very moist; eastward it was arid and rather barren. And here was the end of tidewater; upriver the Columbia no longer responded to the ocean tides.

Skilled Indian paddlers or French-Canadian boatmen were sometimes able to shoot the Cascade rapids successfully, particularly during spring freshets, but customarily even the most daring disembarked and portaged their cargoes. Prior to the building of the Barlow road in 1846, all travelers seeking passage to the lower Columbia or Willamette valleys halted at The Dalles, dismembered their wagons, loaded them upon rafts, and, steering the rude barges down the Columbia to the Cascades, docked at the rapids and portaged wagons and goods around the dangerous white water. Ropes, used as shore lines, guided the rafts to safety. Later the Federal Government built locks at the Cascades, and still later, the present dam. The submerged locks even now are visible. Nard Jones's novel, *Swift Flows the River,* is based on the steamboat era of the Columbia, centering about the Cascades.

Through the years, fishing Indians from the coast and hunting Indians from the east came here to barter, to fish, and to gamble. The Chinookan Indians who occupied the midstream islands just below the rapids harassed all travelers. Only Dr.

John McLoughlin, chief factor at Fort Vancouver, maintained unmolested passage for his traders and trappers; he did it through strict discipline.

From earliest time these Indians were noted for their ugly and thievish natures. Lewis and Clark, on their return from the mouth of the Columbia, noted, "the Wahclellahs (Chinooks) we discovered to be great thieves . . . so arrogant and intrusive have they become that nothing but our numbers saves us from attack . . . We were told by an Indian who spoke Clatsop that the Wahclellahs had carried off Captain Lewis's dog to their village below. Three men well armed, were instantly dispatched in pursuit of them, with orders to fire if there were the slightest resistance or hesitation. At the distance of two miles they came within sight of the thieves, who, finding themselves pursued, left the dog and made off. We now ordered all the Indians out of our camp, and explained to them that whoever stole any of our baggage, or insulted our men, should be instantly shot."

Washington Irving, in writing of Robert Stuart's passage of the rapids in 1812, calls the Cascades "the piratical pass of the river."

On all sides around the Cascades there are objects of natural and historic interest. Lofty crags, often streaked with snow, reach skyward; perhaps the most impressive of these is Table Mountain, on the north shore of the river near the old locks. Just below the locks, on the north side also, stood the old blockhouse built by a young lieutenant in 1856—Phil Sheridan.

"Bridge of the Gods"

One of the most famous of the Columbia River Indian legends was the story of a great natural stone-arch bridge that once spanned the river at the Cascades; this is the theme of Frederic Homer Balch's classic *Bridge of the Gods*. Apparently all the tribes along the Columbia agreed that the river once placidly flowed here through a tunnel or under an arch of stone, and that during a "shaking of the earth" it crashed into the river, making the treacherous Cascades. The Klickitat version of this legend unites both the physical conformation of the Cascades and the three great snow mountains of Hood, Adams, and St. Helens, with the origin of fire:

There was once a father and two sons who came from the east down the Columbia to the region in which The Dalles is now located, and there the two sons quarreled as to who should possess the land. The father, to settle the dispute, shot two arrows, one to the north and one to the west. He told one son to find the arrow to the north and the other to find the arrow to the west, and there to settle and bring up their familes.

The first son went north to what was then a beautiful plain, where he became the founder of the Klickitat tribe; the other son went west to the Willamette Valley, where he became the founder of the great Multnomah nation. To separate the tribes the Great Spirit raised the chain of the Cascades, but without any great peaks, and for a long time everything was peaceful between the tribes. For convenience, the Great Spirit built the tomanowas bridge, under which the waters of the Columbia flowed, and to guard the bridge he stationed a witch called Loowit. She was also to take charge of the sacred fire, then the only fire in all the world. Taking pity on the Indians without fire, Loowit besought the Great Spirit to permit her to give the Indians fire. The Great Spirit granted her request, and to show his appreciation of her kindness granted her great beauty. Then all the chiefs fell in love with the guardian of the bridge, but she paid little heed until finally there came two chiefs, one from the north called Klickitat and one from the west called Wy'east. She could not make up her mind between the two, and this made the two chiefs very jealous.

At last they entered a desperate war and all the land was ravaged. The Great Spirit repented that he had allowed Loowit to bestow fire on the Indians and determined to undo all his work. He broke down the tomanowas bridge, which dammed up the river with an impassable reef, and put to death Loowit, Klickitat, and Wy'east. But because they had once been noble and good, he gave them fitting memorials after death. Over them, as monuments, he raised three beautiful snow mountains, the "Guardian Peaks of the Columbia." Over lovely Loowit, he raised the near-perfect cone of Mount St. Helens; over Chief Wy'east, the lofty splendor of Mount Hood; and over Chief Klickitat, the yellow and vermilion crags of Mount Adams.

According to modern scientists, an adequate support for such a bridge existed only on the north side of the river, and a natural bridge wide enough to span the river would have been structurally impossible. Still, there is every evidence that an enormous rock avalanche once came from the breaking away of an immense volume of the mountains now represented by Table Mountain and Red Bluffs, and that this rock slide more than obstructed the river by a natural dam. It actually buried the old channel and forced the river up on an adjacent rocky bench and over against the mountains bordering the south side of the valley. During geological explorations for the site of Bonneville Dam, surveyors found evidences of the old river bed north of the present channel.

Lewis and Clark, on both their journey out and their return trip, were impressed by the sight of many large trees there, standing erect in about thirty feet of water. In 1835, Samuel Parker concluded that there had been a landslide here "more than twenty miles in length, and about a mile in width." In 1843, Peter H. Burnett, an attorney and later a member of the Oregon Legislature, first saw the Cascades of the Columbia. In his *Recollections of a Pioneer* (1880), he wrote:

"There was then an Indian tradition that, about a hundred years before, the Cascades did not exist, but that there was a succession of rapids from The Dalles to where the Cascades are now . . . This tradition said that the river gradually cut under the mountain until the projecting mass of huge stones and tough clay slid into the river and damned up the stream to the height of some thirty feet, thus producing slack water to The Dalles."

There is today a Bridge of the Gods but it is a cantilever toll bridge spanning the river just west of the old Cascade Locks.

Upriver from the locks are Shell Rock Mountain on the Oregon side and Wind Mountain on the Washington side. The Indians believed that the Great Spirit set the whirlwinds blowing in constant fury about Wind Mountain as a punishment to those who, breaking the taboo, had taught the white men how to snare salmon. There are still evidences of Indian sites near the mouth of Wind River on the north shore, and near Bingen. There was at one time a village at the mouth of the Klickitat River and another two miles up river.

Beyond is Mitchell Point overhanging the river. The great projecting rock was known to the Indians as the Little Storm King, while the sky-sweeping mountain above was called the Great Storm King. Before reaching The Dalles, you will pass Hood River on the south bank and historic White Salmon on the north shore. Just below The Dalles is the lower Memaloose Island, an Indian burial place for untold centuries.

The Long Narrows

The obstructions beginning at Big Eddy at the foot of The Dalles and continuing for five miles upstream to the site of Wakemap Mound, on the north shore, were even more formidable than the Cascades. This part of the river was the "Long Narrows," generally called the Grand Dalles or simply the Dalles; also occasionally Five Mile Rapids. The "Short Narrows" or Ten Mile Rapids was between Brown's Island and the Oregon shore, just below Celilo. Celilo was also called Fifteen Mile Rapids.

In the Long Narrows the river waters were suddenly narrowed and deepened by a rock chasm scarcely more than two hundred feet across. Indians by the thousands, from the north and south and east and west, once came here to fish and trade. They held rendezvous and had great salmon feasts, and the cultures of many different tribes intermingled.

Before it was buried under water of The Dalles dam, the Long Narrows was the most interesting part of the river for any kind of Indian study. I am not sure but that it may be the most interesting Indian ground in the United States. Here the river cut through a hard basalt bedrock, causing many falls, rapids, and eddies. During low water the river was bordered with great stretches of washed bedrock which is very rough and hard to get about in. During the different stages of flood there were many side channels through which the waters rushed. It was an ideal place for taking salmon by the Indian's methods of spearing or dipping. Salmon could be easily netted in the backwaters and quiet eddies as they rested during their fight upstream in the turbulent churning waters. There was no other place in this western country so important as a fishing ground to the Indians as this piece of river.

There was one small, permanent village here—Wishram—but during the salmon season camps were everywhere along the banks where the water level permitted. The high spots on the bedrock were covered with caches of dried fish. The smell of the whole place may have been pleasing to the olfactories of an Indian, but it certainly was the opposite to the white man.

The great yearly gatherings and the permanent village life naturally enriched the adjoining sandy grounds. The number of relics removed from here can only be guessed at. Even the Indians of later days, when they found the whites would buy them, hunted for arrowheads. The country about here is now well picked over, but there is plenty left underground; and there are quite rich spots, no doubt, if we could get to them.

Near The Dalles, on the Oregon side of the river, is an ancient Indian camp site which proved to be one of the richest in Indian relics. It was called the "Bead Patch" by Robert H. Miller, who comes as near to being an authority on the site as anyone I know. I will let him tell firsthand of the "finds" he himself made there and those he saw others make:

The Bead Patch

The "Bead Patch" is a name given affectionately to a low mound of sand and rock lying on the high volcanic rock shore of the Columbia River, just downstream from The Dalles Bridge. I say affectionately advisedly, because when one has experienced the thrills of collecting Indian artifacts, he would surely have a lasting fondness for a camp site which has yielded so many rare stone articles as the Bead Patch has, especially along the line of stone beads and ornaments.

The writer is indebted to Mr. Luhr Jenson, of Hood River,

one of its discoverers, for a visit to the site. During eight years, working at odd times, I have had the pleasure of "screening out" more than 135 linear feet of stone beads of many sizes, in addition to numerous other artifacts.

The camp site is located in a depression of the rocky shoreline, but many years of occupation and the accumulation of camp dirt have raised it so that it is now about eight feet above the surrounding rock, making a mound some fifteen feet higher than when it was first settled. Holes have been dug eight or ten feet deep with no sign of base rock. When screening was commenced, the mound was from two hundred to two hundred and fifty feet across the top, with absolutely nothing to give the least clue to the rare and artistic artifacts it contained. Its discovery was due to the "wash" of an extremely high rise in the river a number of years ago—so high that it left a two-foot log stranded near the top of the mound and undoubtedly washed the lower edge, uncovering the chippings of agate and obsidian which were found throughout the dirt.

The main reason for believing that this camp site was occupied for many years is that the area was built up rather than blown out, despite the strong and prolonged wind storms characteristic of the Columbia river in this section. Numerous lodges banked with hundreds of large stones, many weighing from fifty to two hundred pounds, must have built up a barrier against the winds. People now living along the river in this section are often forced to use screens of brush, boards, or other material to keep their crops from blowing out of the ground.

A peculiar condition existed on this camp site at the time screening was started. A covering of white sand, from twelve to twenty-four inches deep, was found intermixed with the large wall rocks and the smaller stones. A plausible reason for this is that the campground had been built up by many years of occupancy to a height that permitted the wind to strike it sufficiently hard to prevent the burnt substances and clay from further upbuilding. The sand blows back and forth with the changing winds but the finer dust does not return. It was in

The "Bead Patch," just downstream from The Dalles bridge . . . At this ancient village campsite they seemed to specialize in making stone beads. These varied in size from three inches in length to some so small that when strung it would take eighteen or twenty to make an inch. The author could account for more than 20,000 beads from this site of about two acres.

The author and Mr. Miller at work.

Close-up of small stone fish carving.

these top two feet that most of the large beads and artifacts were found.

Neither in the great number of large stones scattered throughout the lower fire dirt, nor in the top stratum as described, is there any indication of what type of abode was used by the inhabitants. There are no wooden stumps left in the ground to indicate that pole and brush houses had been used; and the lack of deer or elk bones in the camp dirt would indicate that the inhabitants had few hides to make tepees similar to those made by some of the latter-day Indians. There were either few of these animals in the immediate vicinity, or the Indians were unable to kill them. Bones of all kinds will remain and retain their form for many hundreds of years, especially so in the light sandy soil found on this camp site. Broken needles, a spear barb, a chipping tool, and a round bird-bone hair holder were the only artifacts made of bone that were found, as far as I was able to ascertain. I am led to believe that the inhabitants must have used a dugout dwelling, with a low stone wall surrounding it, and with a roof of poles and brush or grass covering it. The poles would have been held down with the heavy stones on the outside of the wall.

The tools used to secure the treasures of the Bead Patch were a shovel and several screens of different mesh. Screens of many sizes and shapes have been used here, but the most efficient one is a double box swinging on four legs with a hinge on the top box. A half-inch screen on top catches the large rocks which can then be dumped. Sometimes large beads were found in the top screen, so I always took care to look it over. The smaller rocks, sand, and little beads drop into the next lower screen, which is generally quarter-inch mesh. This second screen catches the medium-sized beads and rocks. Then the small beads, small rock, and the chippings are all stopped by a one-eighth-inch screen. It is a very small stone bead that will go through such a fine screen, but I have picked up a number that have done so.

What happened to the inhabitants of the Bead Patch is a puzzling question. They might have moved away because of high water or for other reasons, but there are no marks of confusion on the site. It is undoubtedly true that it was the custom in ancient times to bury the deceased person's possessions with the body; but there are not enough of the possessions of even a few Indians left to show that the inhabitants died in the usual, natural way. It would seem that in some unremembered time they must have vacated the area, taking most of their possessions with them. The artifacts, numerous as they are, constitute but a small part of those made on this campground, as verified by the broken tools left there.

Some authorities believe that, because of the large number of beads found there, a more recent burial ground might have covered the earlier camp site. Several older Indians living a short distance from the Bead Patch visited with me while I was working the site. They expressed as much surprise as I did when the rare artifacts were screened out. Following are some of the more interesting among the thousands of artifacts found there, with comments on their appearance and use.

Beads: Most of the beads were made of a greenish slate stone but some were of common gravel. The smallest beads varied in size from an eighth to one-fourth inch in diameter, and from paper-thin to an eighth-inch in thickness. When strung together, they averaged from eighteen to twenty-two per inch. Four linear feet of these screened out in one day was the best record.

There were some flat beads from a quarter-inch to one inch in diameter, but these were not numerous. There were tubular beads that varied from a quarter-inch to two inches in length, and from three-eighths to a half inch in diameter, but these were not picked up in quantity either. Most of the tubular beads were of a reddish-brown stone similar in texture to slate. There was also a limited number of square-shaped beads made of greenish-colored slate and ranging in size from one quarter to one half inch in diameter and from two to four inches in length.

The prettiest and best-shaped beads were of a fine-grained blue-black stone called steatite, which, although a comparatively soft stone, takes a high polish. These beads had rounded ends and varied from three-eighths to seven-eighths of an inch in length and from one-quarter to three-eighths of an inch in diameter. There were also some irregularly shaped steatite beads that were roughly flat and ranged from one-fourth to three-fourths inch in diameter; and some tubular beads of steatite and a whitish colored slate. These latter beads were seven-sixteenths of an inch long and three-sixteenths of an inch in diameter. They show how small a bead of this shape could be made. There were also a few beads and bangles of graphite in irregular shapes and sizes, generally about one-fourth to a half inch in diameter.

A few brown beads were found that closely resemble a fine-grain wood. The material must be a kind of stone, otherwise it would be hard to account for the beads retaining their shape and color during the many years they were in the ground. The material itself is very light in weight.

To compute the number of beads taken from this camp site seems almost a hopeless task. During the eight years that I worked there, off and on, many people were "screening." Some found a few beads, while others were lucky enough, or worked hard enough, to find many. Making as careful an estimate as possible from definite knowledge and allowing a fair amount on indefinite reports, I would figure that over one thousand linear feet of stone beads have been taken from this camp site during that time, and I believe my estimate is under, not over, the total number.

The preparation of the stone used in making the different sized beads entailed considerable labor, even though most of the material used was of a semi-soft nature. For the small, flat pieces, it was necessary to cut strips of the stone with stone knives and rub the strips smooth with a sandstone rubbing rock until they were of the desired thickness. Then they were cut into roughly square pieces, perforated with the stone drills, and strung on fine slivers of wood. Finally, the rough corners were rubbed off with a piece of sandstone. The fine scoring done by this process can still be seen on the edges of the pieces with the aid of a magnifying glass.

The method of drilling the holes in the different beads is

Stone bangles and . . .

. . . Some small carved objects for personal adornment.

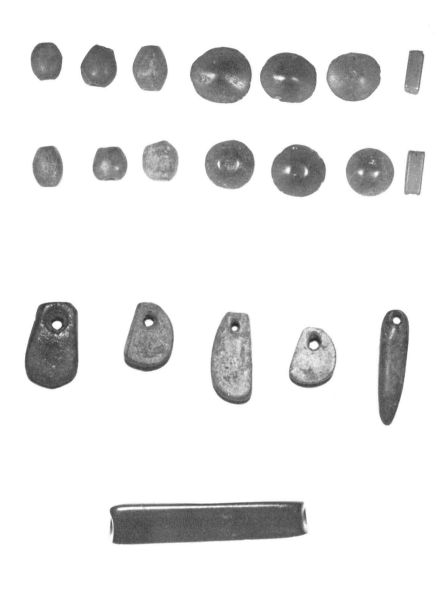

Stone beads and bangles.

open to question because of the fact that two types of drills or drill points have been found. Yet, judging from the hundreds of whole and broken drills that were made to be used while held between the thumb and fingers, this was the type of drill most generally used—even though the number of beads was so large. The reason that some use of other methods is considered probable is based on the fact that drill points with flattened ends have been found. These were set into the end of a stick and rotated by the "bow and string" or the "up and down" rotation method.

Judging from a number of "blanks" drilled and partly drilled, it would seem that the larger beads were shaped to size and then perforated. The opposite seems to have been the case with the small beads. But, in the making of, say, a half-inch-long steatite oval bead, the hole drilled at one end would sometimes accidentally run out the side near the opposite end. Because the bead was so small, also the hole in the side, the lack of alignment was sometimes not noticed until the bead was strung. To remedy this, the worker drilled a hole in the center of the opposite end, to make it line up with the first hole. This time the string was inserted from the opposite end to make the bead hang properly.

Bangles: Some large flat bangles—to be used as ornaments for the arms or ankles—were of white slate and measured from one to three inches in diameter. A number of these had such a large hole cut out that there was more hole than stone. There were many bangles in round and diamond shapes made of brown-and-black fine-grained slate and measuring from one to three inches across the flat face. These have an incised line around the edge to hold a cord for suspension and are one-fourth to one-half inch in thickness.

A most peculiar bangle was made of obsidian in the shape of an oval arrow point with a flat base. It is one and five-eighths inches long, with regular chipping, but the sides of the bangle show unmistakable smoothening with an abrasive. The opening is chipped at direct right angles with the sides. What induced the savage artist to do the hard work necessary to make such

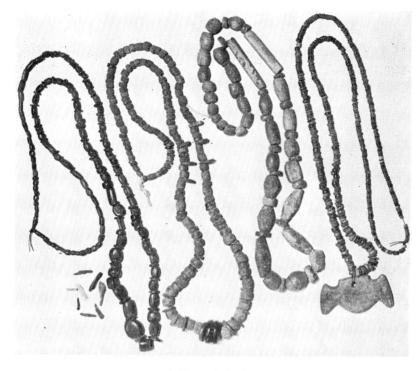

Indian-made beads.

Three-inch pendant.

an opening is hard to imagine. Another odd piece is made of a five-ounce chunk of silver and lead ore and formed into a half-round shape. A hole near the center and a notch cut around the top oval complete what was earlier thought to be a bangle. Recent investigations, though, indicate this was an atlatl weight rather than a bangle.

Nose Ornaments: Not many nose ornaments were found, but some measuring two to three inches were mistaken for broken drills. These pieces, made of agate, obsidian, and other stones, showed that some effort had been made to smooth the chipping by taking off the high points so as not to irritate the nose when worn.

Ear Ornaments: Ear ornaments found were from an inch to an inch and a half in length and about three-sixteenths inch in diameter at the large end, then chipped to a point. No perforated ones were found but the drops were sometimes fastened in the ear perforations with a cord. A semi-hard green slate was used in making them and no other color of stone was used for this purpose. It is a peculiar point, but the Indians of early historical times used the same colored stone and shaped them similarly.

Pendants: Bracelet-shaped pendants of black slate give evidence of the inhabitants' artistic abilities. On a few of these pieces, deeply incised lines were cut on all four sides and perforated here and there as though to add "drops," as we would call them. The size varies little, being from one and a half by two inches to one and three-fourths by three inches in diameter. They were probably hung on a string from the neck as an ornament, since the size of the openings would prohibit their use as bracelets.

Pipes: Several tubular pipes were screened out measuring from six to seven inches in length and from one and a half to two inches in diameter. Some were rubbed smooth, and a few were ornamented on the bowl part with a sawtooth design. Care was taken in the spacing of the "points" to make them uniform. A fine-grained reddish-brown slate, similar to that of

Stone ring pendants.

some of the large beads, was used. No small pipes like those made by the latter-day Indians were found.

War Club Heads: War club heads found at the Bead Patch are entirely different from those occurring on camp grounds of the Indians now living in the same locality. They are from five to six inches long and from one and three-fourths to two inches in diameter, nicely smoothed, and beveled toward the ends, with a groove around the center. There is no "tie" groove cut like the ones made in the round war club heads of the later Indians. Small war club heads that were meant to be encased in a long buckskin sack and fastened to a short stick were plentiful and give a clew to the inhabitants' probable method of fighting.

Tomahawks: One of the finest tomahawks that I have ever seen came from this camp. Made from a "stringer" of rock that is often found in rotten quartz ledges, it is much harder than flint and has a finish as hard as glass. In color it is a mixture of light and dark brown, blue and pink.

Drills: Drills were screened in many sizes and lengths, and from many different kinds of stone, including obsidian, several colors of flint, jasper, and agate. The drills used to perforate the small beads had flat handles, half an inch to an inch in diameter, with needle-sharp points from a quarter-inch to an inch and a half in length. These drills were held in the fingers. Those for the larger beads had flat handles an inch or two in diameter with points from one to three inches in length and a diameter from three-sixteenths to a quarter-inch. One drill point used for making holes in pipes was four inches long and three-eighths of an inch in diameter.

Reamers: Reamers that were used to enlarge the bowls of pipes were made of the same stone as the drills, but had a "widened" point, thereby saving much time in doing that part of the work. The enlarging and shaping of the bowls was done by moving a small stone knife up and down, then reaming the bowls smooth with a piece of sandstone. The up-and-down scratches as well as those made by the reamers can be clearly seen.

Arrow- and Spearheads: Hundreds of arrow points have been

screened out. They vary in length from half an inch to two inches in length. For the most part, they were neatly made, with some of them comparable to the celebrated Columbia River art points made by the latter-day Indians. The spear points were also well made; these vary in length from three to six inches and occur in several colors of agate and obsidian.

Atlatl Weights: Several of these weights, used in stick and spear throwing, were found. Some were made of a common hard sandstone, but a few were of red or black rock. They are neatly shaped and polished and have the regularly placed incision for attaching to the thrower.

Arrow Straighteners: A number of these doughnut-shaped artifacts were picked up. Made of rough volcanic rock three and a half to four inches in diameter, and about an inch in thickness, they were used to straighten the wooden arrows—according to older latter-day Indians and experienced archeologists.

Arrow Smoothers: Compared with other camp sites, there was a surprising lack of this kind of artifact.

Knives: Knives have been found in many shapes and sizes; and of a number of different stones. The general size would indicate that they were meant to be held in the fingers as few would lend themselves to convenient insertion or fastening in wood or bone handles. There was evidently good reason for this, with the lack of both wood and bone at the Bead Patch. A few of the knives reached four inches in width and six or seven inches in length. Several had double blades.

Scrapers: Scrapers, used for smoothing different artifacts, were few and small, but nicely chipped and shaped. The need for this kind of a tool must not have been great for it could have been easily satisfied from the abundance of agate and obsidian scattered through the camp site.

Adzes: A few adz blades, or celts, were found, or, rather, pieces of them. To my knowledge there has not been an unbroken celt found on this camp site. The pieces were of excellent workmanship and of the hardest stone.

Mortars and Pestles: Many bowls and pestles were picked up, most of them neatly made from large river stones. Their diameter varies from six to nine inches. One was nicely decorated with two wavy lines up and down and around the side, and still retained traces of the red and green paint with which it had been covered. Part of a bowl, made of lava rock, about twelve inches high and fourteen inches across the top, was the most ornamental. A line was cut around near the top and another near the bottom; these lines were connected with each other by means of deeply incised lines about four inches apart.

Most of the pestles were plain round cylinders of stone, ranging in size from one inch in diameter and from four to six inches in length up to two inches in diameter and seven and eight inches in length. Some of the smaller ones have flaring tops and a few incised lines up and down the sides. Beaver heads on two or three were similar to those made by the latter-day Indians. Some had enlarged bottoms and small hand grips at the top. Part of the stone used was as soft as slate and of different colors, some of volcanic origin. One was made of a dark red stone as hard as granite.

Metates and *Manos*: Several *metates* or mortars, so common in Fort Rock Valley, were picked up; but no *manos* or grinding stones such as are usually found where *metates* are more numerous. One *metate*, about two feet in diameter, has a small depression pecked near the edge to hold the berries, seeds, or grain to be ground, and a larger and deeper depression near the center for a grinding place.

Paint Pots: Paint pots were plentiful, two and a half to four inches in diameter. They were neatly rubbed smooth and a few had incised lines up and down the sides.

Indian Paint: Indian paint was found in small lumps scattered throughout the sand. Yellow, green, red, and white were found. One piece of red paint had hardened into a soft stone, yet it probably has as strong a color as when made. It is round in shape and flattened into a cake about two inches in diameter and one inch in thickness. Another cake of paint screened out was roughly three-sided in shape, about four inches on each angle, and one and a fourth inches thick. It was a bright brick-red color, and had been so long in the sand that it was thoroughly dried out and granulated. However, when it was rubbed between the fingers it turned to fine powder. From the shape and angles, the cake had been originally about eight inches in diameter.

Carved Figures: These were found measuring from one and a half to two and a half inches in length. Some were straight and some were slightly curved, resembling to a certain degree the form of a salmon, though they had a round body, with a circumference of only a fourth to three-eighths of an inch. Eyes, mouth, and fins were cut in to make the resemblance clearer. Several carved-stone heads were also found, including a monkey head and a baboon head. These are shown on pages 185 and 186.

Two of the finest specimens of stone carving ever found along the Columbia River country were "screened out" on this camp ground. They are in the shape of birds, and one is much more artistically carved than the other as may be seen by referring to the pictures here. The one shown in three views was dug up from a depth of six feet. In size it is two and five-sixteenths inches long, and one and a quarter inches wide, with a circumference of ten to sixteen inches.

The plainer bird was found in the sand and rocks at a depth of about three feet; this, however, is not a clew to the depth it might have been dug up from, as the ground had then been worked over to a depth of six feet. It shows the same skillful work on the head and body. It is slightly larger than the other bird, being two and seven-sixteenths inches long and one and five-sixteenths inches wide, with a body circumference of eleven to seventeen inches. Both birds are made of the same greenish steatite as many of the beads.

Petroglyphs: In addition to these carvings, several stones were found bearing pecked-out figures similar to those on stones and cliffs farther up the river. One of these is a neatly outlined face with some ornamentation; this was found on the top end of a river boulder about four feet long, and might have been used as an idol. Roughly round and rather bulbous

Side, back, and under views of carved stone bird—"fancy."

Carved stone bird—"plain."

at the base, it tapers slightly toward the top where the face is outlined.

Another carving was on a stone about two feet long by ten inches wide, with a thickness of five inches. The design was a large "eye" on one end and a series of lines at right angles to the length of the stone.

Sinkers or "Lead" Stones: Strange as it seems to those who have found many specimens of this artifact on nearly every Indian camp site situated on rivers in which salmon "run," not a girdled or perforated sinker was found in the Bead Patch. A "lead" itself is a woven willow fence extending from deep water up into shallow water and held to the river bed by the sinkers. The salmon following the "lead" gradually swim into the shallower water where they are scooped out with woven willow mats or killed with clubs. It is possible that these ancient Indians might not have used them, and a glance at the river bed at this point would show why. Here the bed of the river is an extension of volcanic rock ledges of the shoreline, and it is so irregular that it would be impossible to install a "lead" to guide salmon into a trap. Another factor that may have been the cause of their non-use here is that the main channel of the river is on the north side and there is no regular current on the south bank.

Salmon Clubs: A number of these rough tools for killing salmon were found. Measuring sixteen to twenty inches in length, they served the same purpose as the light balmwood clubs in use by many present-day Indians. Few of the "screeners" noticed them.

Fish Hooks: The few fish hooks screened out were made of obsidian in the shape of a letter V, with a rounded base and half-inch prongs. While in use, the line was tied to one prong and the bait placed on the other. When swallowed by a fish, the point would catch in its throat and work nearly as efficiently as the white man's hook.

Fish Scalers: Fish scalers by the hundreds were screened out. They were made by taking a small flat gravel stone and chipping off the edge all the way around on one side. These scalers give a definite clew to the source of the food supply of the Indians who lived on this camp site. These artifacts are sometimes called cobble choppers.

Net Measurers: These were not plentiful. Possibly many of the "screeners" were interested only in the beads or arrow points and did not know or care about these artifacts.

Canoes: The use of canoes on the river was almost a necessity to secure the salmon; and, from the number of scrapers found at the Bead Patch, salmon would seem to have been their principal food. However, there are no trees large enough or otherwise suitable for making canoes nearer than forty or fifty miles from this camp site. It must be assumed, then, that these Indians purchased their canoes farther down the river from other tribes, or were compelled to make a trek to the forests and manufacture their own. The lack of tools suitable for this work seems to prove that the work was done elsewhere. Another reason for believing that the inhabitants at the Bead Patch had few canoes is the general absence of pumice rubbing stones for smoothing the wood of canoes. Only two or three of these stones were picked up, which is surprising in an Indian camp so near a river.

Farther up the Long Narrows is Celilo, as well known for its fishing as the Bead Patch is for its beads.

Celilo

Celilo, at Celilo Falls, was a canoe portage as old as the fishing stations held by the Indians under a treaty granting exclusive and perpetual fishing rights to these spots. Long before Lewis and Clark passed here, fishing stands on these rocks were handed down by the Indians from father to son. Robert Stuart of the Astorians writes in his *Journal*: "Here is one of the first rate Salmon fisheries on the river . . . the fish come this far by the middle of May, but the two following months are the prime of the season – during this time the operator hardly ever dips his net without taking one and sometimes two salmon, so that I call it speaking within bounds when I say that an experienced hand would catch at least 500 daily . . ."

Early photo showing where the railroad crossed the Columbia near Celilo . . . This view was taken from the hills to the south. Note the many waterfalls and rapids that made it such a wonderful place for fishing by the Indian methods. Now the area is completely covered by backwaters of The Dalles dam.

Horseshoe Falls on the Oregon side of the Columbia River at old Celilo . . . The platforms built out over the water were standing places to be used in dipping for salmon.

Lewis and Clark reported seeing "great numbers of Stacks of pounded Salmon neetly preserved in the following manner, i.e. after suffi(ci)ently Dried it is pounded between two Stones fine, and put into a speces of basket neetly made of grass and rushes better than two feet long and one foot Diamiter, which basket is lined with the Skin of Salmon Stretched and dried for the purpose, in this it is pressed down as hard as possible, when full they Secure the open part with the fish Skins across which they fasten th(r)o the loops of the basket that part very securely, and then on a Dry Situation they Set those baskets . . . thus preserved those fish may be kept Sound and sweet Several years."

Just what may have been the history of this wonderful place I do not know. What wars or battles may have been fought are hidden in the past, but at the coming of the white man a *status quo* existed which permitted the Indians of many tribes to gather here in peace.

The early photograph showing the old railroad gives a good idea of the great stretches of barren bedrock exposed on both sides of the river along here, before the area was flooded by waters of the dam. Geologists may be interested in noting how the fault—still visible—causing the center falls extends across the country to the north. Up until recent years, you could still find hundreds of petroglyphs on the rocks, and you could lose yourself in the great stretches of washed bedrock. Even the Indians would tell you "Indian legends." If they didn't know one they could tell one anyway—for a price.

Note the island in the photograph of Horseshoe Falls. In the old days no Indian could fish from it; it was taboo. The island was called "The Bear," and there was a rather strange custom connected with it. When a girl was coming into womanhood, she was placed out on this island and left there four days without food or shelter, that she might ponder on the seriousness of the life ahead of her. If she came through this trying ordeal in good condition, she would have "long life."

A few Indians still live at Celilo but the tribal fishing rocks lie under the huge, quiet reservoir behind The Dalles Dam.

Indian village at Celilo Falls.

This stone bowl, found near Celilo on the Columbia, was carved from granite and is nine inches across. In workmanship, it is one of the best to come from the river. It was washed out of a gravel bank after the reservoir behind The Dalles dam was filled.

Since no current is left, the salmon do not come into the eddies where the Indians can dip them. There is much complaint from the Indians who had prized fishing spots downstream from the falls at Celilo.

The young Wyams are moving away, and the age-old customs and traditions of these river people are dying out. Chief Tommy Kuni Thompson, long-time leader of the Wyams, rests in the tribal burial ground above the Columbia; his family is scattered. There is no need nowadays to make a portage around The Narrows, or, for that matter, around the Cascades—two of the most treacherous areas in the mighty river.

Tenino

The Teninos were a small tribe whose territory was a short piece of the south side of the Columbia between The Dalles and Celilo. They were surrounded by the Wasco Indians, and they must have been quite forceful from the respect shown them by the other Indians. Charlie Pitt, an interpreter and the most learned and interesting Indian I have ever met, told me that the Tenino language had but a few hundred words and was most difficult to understand. To learn it, he had to live with the Teninos for two years.

The only petroglyphs showing geometric figures that I have found on the river are in Tenino country. Their stories also seem different. They do not run so much to the immoral as do many of the other river tales, especially those of the Wishrams, who were just across the river. I tell you the following briefly, making no attempt to repeat the Indian's language or many signs. It was told me by a middle-aged Indian who asked me, in all seriousness, if our people knew of any such stones or if we thought this could be true:

In the long time ago the Teninos found a round stone about a foot in diameter that gave off light. They set it up in the village, and it lighted the camp at night. The Wishram Indians across the river became very envious, and one night a party of them came across and tried to steal the stone. They got away with it after quite a battle. Some time later the Teninos gathered together their warriors and, crossing over in the night, recovered the stone. Then again, the Wishrams came over in force, defeated the Teninos, and took the stone. By this time the small tribe of Teninos had lost so many men that they could not attempt to fight for their rock, so a small party crossed over on a stormy night and tried to steal it. They had almost reached their canoe with the stone when the Wishrams discovered them. A scuffle took place, and the stone rolled into the river. The water was very deep there, and the Indians could not get the stone out. All summer it lay there in the deep water throwing off its light; but with the next flood, it washed away and was never found again.

Coyote's Canyon

This deep, ragged, natural race in the bedrock below Celilo has a long Indian story or legend connected with it. The gist of the story is that all the good fishing places along the main stream were owned by the rich people. Coyote, out of the goodness of his heart, built the race so the poor people would have a place to take fish.

Coyote may be either a hero or a villain in the many stories of the upper river. West of the mountains the salmon takes his place. An Indian offered to tell me the story of the canyon for three dollars a day. It would take three days to tell it. I didn't accept his offer.

In *Oregon Geographic Names*, Lewis McArthur quotes J. W. Elliott, former superintendent of Warm Springs Indian Reservation, to the effect that this area of the Columbia was known as Tenino Fishery and the name meant a river channel where the water was confined by steep rock walls. When the Tenino Indians were moved to the reservation, they took the name with them, and some of the older ones explained its meaning to Elliott. The picture of Coyote's Canyon shown here could well be the place meant, as it is near the village site of the Tenino Indians. The structures in the distance are fish wheels.

Coyote's Canyon.

Coyote's fishing place.

Coyote's Fishing Place

Many points along the river have legends or stories connected with them. This point of a low cliff in the bedrock at the Tenino village site was an excellent fishing spot when the water was at the right stage. Standing on the point, the fisherman could dip either side. The Indians called it Coyote's fishing place, and they would show you some indentations in the top they said were Coyote's tracks. Some of the carvings were supposed to mark the Indians' family fishing grounds. I did not have any of these carvings pointed out to me, but the two shown here might easily be such.

About the Celilo fishing places, the rapids were so noisy that a person could speak to another only when very close to him and then only by shouting. This led to an odd custom. When a dip netter caught a salmon, he killed it and then laid it with the others at the nearest suitable spot. Any Indian passing and wanting a fish could take one, but if the fisherman were having poor luck and not getting the fish he needed or wanted for himself, he would give his buttocks two slaps, which meant not to take any.

Wishram

The ancient village of Wishram, on the Washington side of the river, was at the head of the Long Narrows and about ten miles below the railroad town of the same name. There, salmon —struggling upriver to their spawning grounds—were caught and dried and packed in bundles and bales of various sizes for trading purposes.

Washington Irving, in his *Astoria*, describes how tribes from the Pacific Coast brought sea food, wappato, and other roots and berries. From the interior, along the Snake and Columbia rivers, they drove in with horses, or paddled downstream in canoes laden with robes, dried meat, and other items to trade.

Here at Wishram, as at Celilo Falls and Tenino, during the great salmon runs, the Indians stood out on the frail scaffoldings, fastened precariously on the rocky sides of the channel above the rapids, with ropes fastened to their waists and long, pointed javelins in hand, awaiting the leap of the salmon. In the split second when the fish were arrested in mid-air, the spears were driven home. Spearing and netting were the two methods used and both required rare skill.

At Wishram, Lewis and Clark wrote: "landed and walked accompanied by an old man to view the falls . . . we arrived at 5 Large Lodges of natives drying and preparing fish for market, they gave us Philburts, and berries to eate."

"Grandma" Spedis

It was here that a friend and I saw the oldest human being I have ever seen. One December I took a trip to Wishram to get pictures of some of the petroglyphs so numerous there. It was cold and windy at the village, and I was glad to be invited to the Spedis family's house. We were warming ourselves, when my companion noticed a pile of blankets on the floor near the wall move a little. After it happened a few times, he spoke of it, and Martin Spedis said,

"Oh, that's just Grandma." He drew the blankets aside and uncovered the head and shoulders of the old lady. He spoke to her in a loud voice, and she drew herself to a sitting position. She was very nearly blind. She was so shrunken that she looked like a mummy. Her people claimed she was almost one hundred and thirty years old. They figured from the arrival of Lewis and Clark, as she had often told of the first white expedition to come down the river.

I asked if she wouldn't tell us something of the early days. She thought a moment and then talked to Martin. He turned to me and said, "She says that when she was a little girl the Indians caught two black men along the river. They were very, very black. The Indians had never seen any people like that before." As that seemed to be the end of her story, I asked what the Indians did with them. She replied to Martin in a few brief words, and he said to me "She says they skinned them."

She was spoken of as "Grandma" or "Old Mary," and they said she slept most of the time. I saw her again about two years later, and she died the following year. The "black men" she referred to would have been Hawaiians or "Kanakas" of the Hudson's Bay Company.

Indian Sweat Bath

This shows the frame, partly covered, of a sweat bath near Wishram. When in use, these baths are entirely covered with mats, and they are always placed close to the water. A pile of rocks is placed in a shallow pit inside the house; then the naked Indian sprinkles water on the rocks, causing the house to fill with hot steam. When he feels he has boiled long enough, he comes dashing out and plunges into the cold water.

This "cure," used in times of plagues of smallpox and measles, was the cause of many deaths. It was largely responsible for the terrible toll that the intermittent fever of the early 1830s took among the Northwest Indians. Some Indians still take this treatment.

Children's Slide

I offer this as being probably the oldest children's slide in America. It is of hard basalt rock and is at the westerly edge of the old Indian village of Wishram. Ages ago the great slanting rock had tumbled down from the cliff above to produce a ready-made slide. Two grooves are worn in the stone by the generations of children who slid down it. If we assume this village to be one of the oldest in the United States, and it may well be, then this slide is indeed old. The grooves would indicate age.

Having known Indian children of years ago, I can assure you that no article of children's apparel had anything to do with the wearing of those grooves. Dirt, sand, and fish grease may have helped considerably. The slide is now under water.

WISHRAM

Top: Indian Village of Wishram. *Center*: Sweat bath. *Bottom*: Children's slide.

97

Wakemap Mound, looking east.

Wakemap Mound

Wakemap Mound, at the site of the Indian village of Wishram, on the north shore of the river, was deserted even when Lewis and Clark passed by, but the area around it was heavily occupied. The age of the mound is unknown and it is a rarity on the Columbia. Countless centuries likely went into the multi-layered refuse heap; how many has not been determined. Members of the Oregon Archaeological Society in recent years have worked the mound to bedrock. Their findings include the usual implements used in the routine of daily life: mortars and pestles and mauls; but elaborate objects were found to be rare. Likely this was because Wakemap Mound was not a burial site where valuable art objects were placed with the dead. Now the mound has practically disappeared under the waters of Lake Celilo.

C. A. Millington

Digging in Wakemap Mound. The upper photo shows the Martin Spedis house in the background.

The Storm Hole

This peculiar hole in a small cliff between The Dalles and Celilo has an interesting significance to the old Indians. It controls the winds and storms, so they think. It must be kept stopped up if you want good weather. If left open the wind will blow, and the rains will come. If water is put in the hole it will surely rain. However, in the hottest part of the summer it is often opened to make days become cooler. Even now, if an old Indian passing by finds that someone has pulled the filling out, he will stop immediately, fill the hole with weeds, and face it with flat stones.

The hole, about ten inches across and deep, appears to be a pot-hole worn in the rock in ancient days when the river was at this high level. Lying horizontal, it was undermined as the river went down, leaving the face perpendicular. There is no evidence of its having been dug out by the Indians.

I have seen so much vandalism that I hesitate to tell exactly where places are, fearing they might be destroyed. The Indians will tell you that Coyote dug the hole and that he put the stone under the piece of cliff to hold it up, as shown in the picture.

"Storm Hole" between The Dalles and Celilo.

The "Storm Hole"—closed.

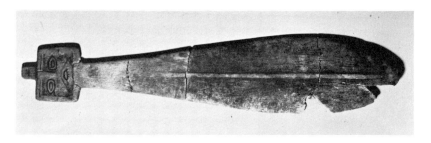

This carved whalebone club was likely traded down from the Northwest Coast. It was found in a prehistoric cremation pit at the Long Narrows; and, like most of these specimens that are discovered, it is badly shattered. The carving is repeated on the reverse side.

The Mouths of the Deschutes and John Day Rivers

These were natural places for Indian camps, and the lands thereabouts have produced numerous relics, as have the large bars on the opposite, or north bank of the river. The Deschutes, often designated on old maps as Falls River, enters the Columbia over a bedrock rapid that makes a good fishing place. Lewis and Clark found that this river, "which is called by the Indians To-wahnahiooks," was "divided by numbers of large rocks, and Small Islands covered by a low growth of timber."

At the mouth of the river, I have been told there was once a small island. The Indians considered it a spot of safety on this more or less dangerous south side of the river, and they made much use of it. They floated firewood and tepee poles of jack pine down from miles above.

In the early part of the last century this island was slowly cut or dissolved away, leaving a gravel bar that is exposed during low water. Some years ago, this bar was the center of operations for a crew of commercial hunters. When I passed it one autumn, about 1926, it looked as if a steam shovel had been at work there. The gravel had been turned over to bedrock and left piled in windrows. Later I saw a collection of about one hundred arrowheads a friend had purchased from one digger. They were all perfect, beautiful specimens. If memory isn't failing me, he paid sixty dollars for the lot.

Miller Island, about three miles long, lies right above the Deschutes. This was the scene of operations for a party of scientific men from the University of California in the summer of that same year. Unfortunately for them, a bad sand storm was on during their entire stay. Knowing what that can mean, I marvel that they stayed a day. I was invited to visit them by the late Henry Biddle, who was assisting the expedition. I passed there on my way to Central Oregon, where I intended to do some relic hunting. Finding the storm progressing, I kept going. Later I enjoyed an evening with W. Egbert Schenke, one of the party. I went over my own collection while listening to an account of their work during the storm, a description of which can be found in *Archaeology of The Dalles-Deschutes Region*, published by the University of California.

The John Day River, called LePage's River by Lewis and Clark for a member of their party, honors a member of the Astorians. Washington Irving, in *Astoria*, describes John Day as "a hunter from the backwoods of Virginia . . . about forty years of age, six feet two inches high, straight as an Indian; with an elastic step as if he trod on springs, and a handsome, open, manly countenance. He was strong of hand, bold of heart, a prime woodsman, and an almost unerring shot." Day, with Crooks and several French-Canadians, fell behind on the Snake River, while Hunt forged ahead with the main party, in the winter of 1811-1812. The following spring when, after many hardships, the two Americans reached the mouth of the John Day River "they met with some of the 'chivalry' of that noted pass, who received them in a friendly way, and set food before them; but, while they were satisfying their hunger, perfidiously seized their rifles. They then stripped them naked and drove them off, refusing the entreaties of Mr. Crooks for a flint and steel of which they had robbed him; and threatening his life if he did not instantly depart." In this forlorn plight they were found months later by a passing party and taken to Astoria. Day decided to return to the States with Robert Stuart's party, but before reaching the

Willamette he became violently insane and was sent back to Astoria where he died within the year.

The mouth of the John Day was never better ground for relics than were many other spots along the south bank. All these small bars were productive clear up to Umatilla. Beyond here for about twenty miles, the cliffs come in close to the river most of the way until one reaches Wallula. I know of a man who collected about three thousand arrowheads along this south shore in the course of several months. About this same time another man was finding quite a few arrowheads by screening for them. He knew nothing about hunting and was shoveling against an eight-foot bank. Somehow he had realized he could find an arrow point once in a while if he screened that sand.

Near what is now called Quinton, I know of a bar that blew out clear to bedrock. It was cleaned of arrowheads. Gradually the sand blew back onto it, until some years later a new bar was formed. That is one bar that will probably be hunted often, but it will produce nothing.

Up river from the mouth of the John Day River, and on the Washington side is Roosevelt, formerly one of the areas richest in Indian petroglyphs; now they are all gone.

The greatest change I ever saw in the Columbia—in pre-dam days—was near Irrigon, just up the river from Roosevelt. There the south bank had built out for over a mile. I once had occasion to look for some meander corners set on the bank in the sixties. On measuring out to their locations, I was surprised to find I was still over a mile from the present river bank. The filling was of gravel, extending some miles along the bank, and was from twenty to thirty feet deep. The new land was covered with sagebrush and appeared no different from the old. You could, however, find the line of the old bank; there were slight depressions in places and other Indian signs to indicate it. Besides, the old bank showed scraps of shell, chippings, and an occasional camp rock, while the new ground was barren of such. I know of some collectors who worked the present shore line for some miles and complained that there was just nothing along it. I believed them.

Harrison Collection
Tube pipes and stone bangles from the mouth of the John Day River.

Petroglyph at Roosevelt, Washington.

105

Petroglyph at Fountain Bar.

Fountain Bar

As I said before, the north bank of the Columbia has produced more relics than the south bank. The sand bars are large and separated by stretches of cliffs that come down close to the water. Some of these large bars have been fairly well blown out; others are intact and so still hold many relics. I will speak of one place in particular, Fountain Bar—about fourteen miles above the mouth of the John Day River—as to me it is the most fascinating.

Lewis and Clark camped here and left a word picture of the location. David Thompson stopped here in 1811, and the Indians gave a dance in his honor. At that time about four to five hundred Indians were living here. It is called Fountain Bar because the Seattle, Portland & Spokane Railroad station of Fountain is located about the center of the bar, which is about two miles long. The entire waterfront shows a heavy occupancy, and the higher back levels naturally accumulated considerable relics.

Some years ago, an elderly friend of mine, while working with an engineering party on the opposite side of the river, recalled seeing immense clouds of sand and dust rising from here and extending upstream for more than a mile. Afterwards I learned that the bar started blowing away in 1893 because part of it had been plowed at the west end. This breaking of the sod in an attempt to farm these dry bars — as well as over-grazing — has, in most cases, caused them to be cut away.

I didn't get to visit this bar till many years later, when I knew, of course, that I had come late. I had, from time to time, heard many stories of collections made here and was sure they were true, for nearly the whole bar had been blown out. At that, I had no cause for complaint. On one small spot, not over twenty by fifty feet in extent, I picked up more than fifty chipped pieces worth keeping. Sand dunes were crawling up and down the bar, and I happened to hit this one spot which had just been uncovered and was unexplored.

A three-day hunt yielded more than two hundred chipped pieces and many stone relics. The arrow points were of many shapes and among the finest. I also found a great many of all kinds of fishing rocks, and at the lower end of the bar I found the remains of leadways of stone to bring the fish in close to the banks. There were petroglyphs at both ends of the bar. This must have been an unusually good fishing place, and a great deal of Indian material must have been washed down the river.

The special camp site spoken of by Lewis and Clark and by David Thompson appears to have been east of the middle of the bar and is mostly blown out down to gravel. The waterfront here is a fine gravel bar with some spots of semi-laminated bedrock standing a few feet above the gravel. It has not changed much since the Indian days, as their signs are indicated by the shallow basins worn in the bedrock. I found some relics in the cracks or layers of the water-worn bedrock, after remarking they would be good places in which to store things.

On a lower part of this bar, I noted with interest a group of burials that were gradually being exposed by the wind. Water

Fountain Bar, cutting away . . .

Fountain Bar, cut away . . . These pictures show the bar at different stages of blowing out. Note how hard spots resist until the last. During the course of cutting away, all heavy aricles will be on the top of the hard ground . . . These pictures also show why hunting has been easier and better on the upper river than west of the mountains, where the ground is covered with grass and brush.

may have helped, too, as they were close to it. This was a narrow place, and it was right among camp sites. How deep these burials had been, I could not tell, but they were all on the same level. In some cases a few ribs would show; in others, a part of a skull. There were, in all, about forty, all buried with their heads upstream. I found no relics about them, but they might not have been exposed yet, or they might have been placed on the surface of the ground. I did not disturb this place, but from a blown-out grave on higher ground, I picked up enough very small pieces of wampum to make a string about six inches in length. Nothing else appeared to have been placed there.

Very few trade beads or other trade articles were evident, but I did find one small piece that caught my attention: Lewis and Clark on their return trip up river were very hard up because their trade goods were all gone. While camped at this village, they searched out a little copper and brass from among their things. This they made into small bangles, and they traded a few for four dogs which they ate the next day. I found a little brass or copper bangle in a triangle shape on this site. It is an inch wide and one-half inch high, and the edges are worn smooth. The hole is punched, not drilled. Somehow I feel that I have one of the Lewis and Clark bangles. I cannot be sure, but the chances are very good.

I had a rather amusing experience at Fountain Bar. On my second trip there I somehow got the impression that the owner—who lived by himself near the railroad station—might object to my hunting. Because I did not want to be bothered with him, when my companion and I got off the train, we threw on our packsacks and struck out down the track. We saw him looking at us, but we kept right on going until we were out of sight. Shortly after making camp in a large grove of willows at the river bank, a sand storm came on; and while it was bad we searched the ground in view of his house, leaving the other places for the quiet times.

In the evening, before the morning we meant to leave, we let ourselves be seen. He was right after us to know what it was all about. We became very mysterious, letting on that we were engineers making some examinations along the river. Then, turning the tables on him, we did the questioning, getting his opinion on everything about a river bar that we could think to ask him, including the price per acre and whether he thought the blown-out sections could be redeemed. He fell for our hoax and concluded we were representing some big company that was planning to irrigate a large tract. He became very cooperative and confided that someone had stuck him with that bar.

When we led around to the subject of Indian relics—which, we said, we had seen a few of on the bar—we had to listen to a long tale of grievances about the trouble he had with people trying to steal his rocks. They would carry them off, even after he had gone to all the work of carrying them above high water. We learned that he had a small collection of light pieces in his house, but he was too lazy to carry in the heavy ones. We arranged to be up at his house in the morning before train time.

He told us when he left that he had hunted for us the last three days but could find only our tracks and not our camp site. We then began to fear that we would have trouble getting away with our relics. We had gathered far more than we could carry, but we meant to get on that train with all we could of the best of them. A lucky notion then struck me and I remarked:

"That fellow isn't going to stop us. He is going to let us take our stuff without trouble; and, more than that, he is going to give us some of his."

The next morning we took our cameras and went up to see his collection. Then I made a speech, laying it on thick, telling him that a man with the foresight and unselfish thought to have gathered those relics—to preserve and care for them for the generations to come—was a patriot and a noble citizen. I didn't know I could let myself go so much until I got into the spirit of it. Well, he carried his rocks out of the house for us to photograph, stood for his own picture, and gave us a few of his specimens we wanted. When the train came, we climbed onto it with about a hundred pounds apiece.

Sand dune at Fountain Bar . . . This picture, showing the river at the bar, shows how the wind eats into the ground ahead of a crawling dune. Any relics that were hidden in the original ground will be on the surface of the pit. This dune was likely somewhere else by the following summer, but another probably took its place . . . Clumps of willows, such as can be seen here, are the best protection against the sand storms which can be very severe along the upper river.

Raking in sand at Fountain Bar before this part of the bar had blown clear out . . . "It was made up of loose sand, and we had to rake to find the rocks, but it was worth it."

Relics picked up on Fountain Bar by the former owner of the land. In the foreground is a Hudson's Bay axe. The long pestle is for salmon packing. On the back row is a "cross pestle," a rare type found along the river. Note the many large canoe anchors.

This man was an exception to the rule. In those early days, you could go where you pleased and feel perfect freedom. People were scarce along the upper Columbia, and the few who were there were always glad to talk to you and tell you all they knew.

At another time, on the lower end of this bar, we saw a man some distance away who was apparently hunting for arrows. He finally drifted over to us, and we saw he was a young Indian. He asked us if we had seen any Indians pass down that way. We said, "no," and then he told us he was from Umatilla and had come to visit his friends living on Rock Creek. They had all gone, he guessed, to Celilo to fish. Two or three times, he remarked, "Me no fish." We couldn't help thinking that it might be beneath his dignity to fish, but he certainly could pick a very opportune time to visit his friends who did fish.

About fifteen miles up the river from Fountain Bar, at a station on the Seattle, Portland & Spokane Railroad called Moonax, is another large sand bar that is almost entirely blown out. Once on a trip there I found the whole place raked into windrows; I also found the burned remains of what had been a fine, large canoe. Other large camp sites between Fountain Bar and Umatilla included Alderdale, Roosevelt, and Blalock Island.

I do not wish to give the impression that these bars are the only good ones along this part of the river; they are merely among the best. Every bar has relics underground if it was large enough for an Indian family to have stood a tepee on.

Blown-out grave at Fountain Bar . . . Where this grave was found the sandy ground had been cut over six feet deep. The stones were placed on the grave to keep coyotes from digging. In the sand we picked up enough wampum to make a string about six inches in length. It was the smallest wampum we ever found, the pieces being only one-fourth inch across, and very thin.

Burial Sites

Lewis and Clark noted several burial places when they came down the Columbia in 1805, but all the Indian dead were not put away at such burial spots. Many graves were made in the talus, the rock debris at the base of a cliff. This was particularly true along the north bank of the Columbia and on the Snake River. But, whatever the mode of burial—cremation, tree and canoe burial, or ground burial—they all left their signs along the rivers, though there is little trace of them now. Following are some of the main ones on the Columbia noted by the first white men.

About ten miles downstream from Wallula, Washington, is a long island which, from its shape, was called Canoe Island. The cemetery was on the extreme east end. The flood of 1894, which was several feet higher than any other recorded high water, must have swept this island rather clean, taking away all wood and all small objects that would float. The burial site has since been cut by the winds, and it is not possible to locate it exactly, but the ground had been picked clean for many years.

Blalock Island

Blalock Island, which was used by the Indians of Fountain Bar, was one of the important sites. The cemetery itself was at the extreme upper end of the island. The last time I visited it, it was covered with drifting sand and all the buildings were gone. One early traveler spoke of the number of horses that had been killed on this island, and I found the low ground covered with their bones.

Part of a burial hut was still standing here on Upper Memaloose Island when this photograph was taken. The basket on the skull does not belong there; it was some- one's idea of a prank. Now all lies under the burial waters of The Dalles dam.

Memaloose Islands

Two other well-known early Indian burial grounds were those of Upper and Lower Memaloose Island; *memaloose* means "death" or "dead." Both of these islands were burial places where

Lower Memaloose Island, looking north toward the Washington shore.

Remains of a burial hut on Lower Memaloose Island . . . Both of these pictures were taken from the top of the island. What remains of the island can best be seen from the Columbia River Highway on the Oregon side of the river.

the dead were put away in houses. Houses were built, and occasionally just platforms; they were filled with the dead, and in time decayed and fell down, and nature was left to take over. In later years the bodies were placed in coffins before being put in the houses; sawed lumber is common among the debris. The proportionate number of flathead skulls gives a good idea of how common this practice was in the early days.

Lower Memaloose is a desolate basalt island a few hundred feet out in the river, just below Lyle, Washington. Until around 1860, the Indians at The Dalles placed their dead, with their possessions, on this island. For years the ground was robbed until, at the building of the Bonneville Dam, the remains were removed.

Lewis and Clark called Lower Memaloose "Sepulchar rock" when they stopped there in the spring of 1806: "We halted a fiew minits at the Sepulchar rock and examined the deposit of the dead at that place . . . Some of them (huts) were more than half filled with dead bodies. there was 12 sepulchars on this rock which stands near the center of the river, and has a surface of about two acres above the water."

On this island and facing south is the large white Trevitt monument commemorating Victor Trevitt, a pioneer of The Dalles, who chose to be buried on the island sacred to his Indian friends. The story goes that, many years ago, three pioneers, John Martin, Amos Underwood, and Vic Trevitt, while drinking in a Dalles saloon, began a discussion of death; they formed a compact to be buried together on the island, Trevitt asserting that he wanted to sleep among honest people. He was the only one of the three whose friends or relatives would honor the agreement; after his death in San Francisco his remains were shipped to Lower Memaloose.

Upper Memaloose Island was in use until the building of The Dalles Dam, when it was found that backwater from the dam would submerge most of the island. At that time the remains of some 2,500 Indians were removed by helicopter and reburied on the Washington side near The Dalles Bridge. Earlier, Congress had set aside this island for the exclusive use of the

Yakima Indians; and it was a federal offense for whites to go on the island. But that did not prevent them; many continued to go there and rob the "big rock."

"Lower Cascades"

Another famous old burial site was just east of North Bonneville, Washington. In early days this would have been called "Lower Cascades," but the dam has destroyed all signs of the cascades which were so important to the Indians when catching salmon. The old portage road, the S. P. & S. Railroad, and the Evergreen Highway all pass through the site. This was once an outstanding vault burial place.

Vault burials may have been made here as late as 1860. Mr. Anton Labbe—one of the three "Labbe brothers," well-known Portland pioneers—told a story about this place: In about 1861, he was working as a cook in a construction camp on the portage road, and the smell from the cemetery was not as fragrant as a rose. One day when the wind was right, some of the workmen set fire to the woods and burned the whole place out.

What I picked up from the surface there all showed the effect of fire. Early travelers had commented on the large number of carved boards standing about the vaults; they, of course, were left in ashes.

When the highway was built, all the skulls and bones scattered about in the brush were gathered and buried in the fills. As far as I know, few stone artifacts were taken from here, although there may have been in earlier time than I have record of. I do know of a few arrowheads and other chipped pieces that were dug out, but most of the material was early-day trade goods, such as beads, sheet copper, and buttons. Also, several numbered Phoenix buttons show that they were scattered over the country before this burial place was discontinued.

I once found a Northwest Token here, but it was so burned and worn that it would not photograph. This medal is nearly the size of a fifty-cent piece, and it is made of brass. On one side is the head of a trapper with a fur hat; beneath is the word "Token." At the bottom is the date 1820. Since this was the year before the North West Company combined with the Hudson's Bay Company, this medal was new when it was given out. On the opposite side is a beaver and around it is inscribed "North West Company." I don't know how many of these tokens were handed out in this territory, but few have come to light.

Among the early travelers who wrote about this burial spot was the Reverend Samuel Parker, who noted in his *Journal of an Exploring Tour (1838)*: "As I continued down the Indian path, at no great distance from the village, I came to several depositories of the dead. These were built of planks split from balsam fir and cedar, about eight feet long, six wide, and five high, and well covered. At one end is what might be called a door, upon which were paintings of various devices, which did not appear to be designed for any other purpose than for ornamentation. Some had paintings on the sides as well as the doors. The number of these depositories I did not ascertain, as many of them were far decayed, as hardly to be distinguishable; but of those in good condition there were eight or ten."

The last burial place often noted by travelers was Mount Coffin on the lower river, which was used for canoe, scaffold, and tree burials. Not a sign is left of these now; vandalism and weather have destroyed everything. For many years there was a quarry at this site.

I once asked an old Indian what the idea was back of vault burials, and I got this answer, "Sometime an Indian die, but maybe he not dead. When we see him rot we know him dead."

Ancient Indian village site on Sauvies Island. The excavation is a test hole made prior to excavations conducted by the Oregon Archaeological Society.

WALLULA MONOLITH—AN OREGON ROSETTA STONE

From left: We-la-lu-tum, an old Wasco warrior; Albert Kokup from Warm Springs, a scout in the Modoc War; Pipe Shear from Satus Canyon, Yakima, then living at Warm Springs; Bill Charley from Celilo; Tulux Holliquilla, a leading Indian of Warm Springs; the author; Louie Brown, an interpreter for the Yakimas. All the old fellows are gone now.

Wallula Monolith

In the courtyard of the Portland City Hall is a large monolith found about five miles west of Wallula on the right-of-way of the O. R. & N. Railroad, about thirty feet south of the track. Changes in the mileage and in the location of the track have made it impossible to find the exact spot now. Back of the stone is an interesting story:

In the spring of 1897, an engineering party with the late J. P. Newell—a well-known consulting engineer of Portland—in charge was working on what was then the O. R. & N. Railroad. They stopped for lunch at the place where the rock was found, and sat on the rock to eat. The top of it was entirely covered with a short moss or lichen, but they noticed a bit of carving and scraped off some of the moss. All joined in and soon they cleaned the entire top of the rock, and Newell even made some sketches in his field book.

On returning to Portland, he gave the location of the stone to the curator of the museum, but nothing was done about it. Years later, a member of the Park Bureau, then in charge of the museum, received a letter from a Mr. Kaiser telling of the stone and its location. The curator wrote to the superintendent of the Railroad and asked if he wouldn't bring the rock to Portland. The superintendent agreed he would—when he had the opportunity. The curator had practically forgotten about it when, one day, he got a phone call saying that the rock was at the yards and would he please take it away as they needed the car. When the curator asked the size of the stone, he was told it probably weighed ten tons; he had had in mind a stone about two feet long. He had no museum money for moving such a load. However, he had it to do, and he hustled around and got a truck to move it to the City Hall.

The stone has since been given a concrete foundation and stood on end. This is wrong, as the original position of the rock was with the carving upward. A close-up photograph appears on page 228.

According to the concensus of the old Indians shown in the picture, this rock was used in the training of the young men. When an Indian boy reached the age when he thought he should be a man, he was put through a course of training to give him strength and courage to teach him to respect his elders. One test of courage was to send him to some marked spot far from the village, where he was required to remain for a day and a night. The spot selected was in the direction of unfriendly neighbors, and this stone marked such a place. The carvings had not been made by the youths staying there, but had been made ages ago and were known to the Indians in that region.

The Oregon Desert

By the desert country I mean that large part of Oregon roughly bounded by the Deschutes River on the west, the John Day River on the north, and southerly and easterly by Nevada and Idaho. I have covered most of this country personally, and the picture I get from my own observations is that Snake Indian relics are scattered over all the region, with concentrations at points where natural conditions suggest they should be. The Snake flint work is rather poor, and the stone work we know little about; in fact, I was never sure it was Snake work when I saw it. These Indians could not have had much, unless some stone work found at such places as Warner Lakes, or Pyramid Lake in Nevada—or in the streams leaving the east side of the Steens Mountain—was theirs. These were places known in later years to have held large populations of Snake Indians.

It is my belief that the Snakes had roamed this country only a few hundred years at the most, and that before them there must have been Indians who were far more advanced in Indian

Noontime on the desert . . . Pick out a large *metate* for a table. Set out your canteen and open a couple of cans. Forget the sun is beating down upon you. If a little sand in your lunch bothers you, you had better stay out of the desert, because you can't get away from sand.

Rattlesnake Cave.

civilization. Signs of this former population will be found in the southeastern part of this country in overhanging caves. The examination of these overhangs is a hot, disagreeable job, but I have done just enough of this to convince me that much is to be learned from them. All that I have examined have been used by Indians. The roofs are usually smoked and some appear to have been mere shelters rather than habitations. Rattlesnake Cave, shown here, is on the west side of Lake Abert. The bottom was covered with about two feet of alkaline dust mixed with sheep leavings and bones. My exploration was not very thorough as I found the place occupied by four big rattlesnakes, which in getting away from us crawled into holes around the bottom of the walls. Their continued buzzing as I threw dirt around was rather distracting.

Geology tells us that the part of Oregon east of the Cascades was once a much wetter country than it is now. We know that it has been drying up so fast since the time of the first whites that it is anybody's guess how long ago it was that many places, now desert, might have been ideal for Indian life.

If you look at an old map, you will find many spots marked lakes that are now alkali or sagebrush flats. Thorne Lake is now a hard, sun-cracked alkali bed; yet Thomas Condon, the geologist, records catching a ten-inch whitefish there in 1876. Christmas Lake has blown away. Fossil Lake has had no water for years, yet one can get water by digging two or three feet into the old bed. A few water holes for stock are kept open this way, but they may disappear in a few more years. Silver Lake, about seven miles long at the time of the first white settlers, is now a hayfield. However, this, as well as several other lakes, was dried up when incoming water was diverted for irrigation. The water table of this whole section of the country has lowered greatly in the last twenty years. I shall not attempt to cover explorations in the whole "Snake" country, but shall give some details regarding one of the locations—the Fort Rock Valley.

Fort Rock Valley

Fort Rock Valley in Lake County, Oregon, is a waterless, sagebrush plain, over a large part of which are scattered, narrow ridges, small and disconnected, and averaging about twenty to thirty feet in elevation above the general level. Apparently they were built by the wind of sand and clay sediment, possibly in ages past when there may have been dry cycles that gave the wind its opportunity. They are now badly cut by wind and rain. Many of these ridges come to an edge at the top, but others widen to a flat level or bench. In other places there are areas of a few acres in extent that are built up a few feet higher than the water level of the lake beds. In past time, Indians occupied all these ridges and benches that appear to have been near a once-existent marsh, and that were otherwise suitable for habitation. The number and extent of such camp sites is surprising.

Long before Mount Mazama exploded, forming a caldron for beautiful Crater Lake, there were Indians in the Fort Rock country. There were wildfowl of many kinds in the valley, even some

This deserted homestead in Fort Rock Valley shows how, in places, the ground has blown out since the homesteaders pulled out the sagebrush. Any shade in this country is surely welcome on an August afternoon. The ground is covered with obsidian chippings and chips from the settlers' juniper woodpile.

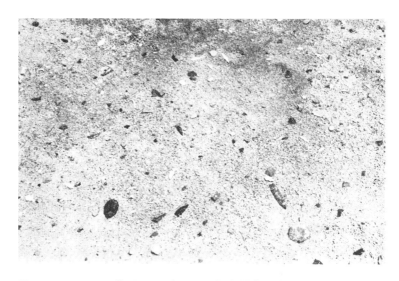

This is a close-up of "rich ground" in Fort Rock Valley, showing how the chipped implements and chippings appear as the ground blows out. This ground was "as is" and was not "salted" for the picture.

flamingoes, the scientists say; and there is even evidence of buffalo along with antelope and deer. Old Fort Rock Lake was a branch of a much larger lake which reached south to cover the entire Silver Lake country of today, spread northeast to cover the area of Thorn Lake and Christmas Lake, and swung north into the Paulina foothills. As the waters dried up, Fort Rock Valley was left as a connected series of lakes and marshes. This condition remained for a long time, and the Indians found it ideal for their living. They occupied it as long as it remained suitable. In the summer of 1938, anthropologists excavated sagebrush-bark sandals from Fort Rock Cave, which have been dated as nine thousand years old.

We can picture this large marsh surrounded by willow, cottonwood, and other trees, the banks lined with wappato and water lily. The drier lands about would have abounded in antelope and rabbits. There would have been waterfowl by the million and whitefish in all the better waters. Timber for canoes would have been available in the forests immediately to the west. I have come across shallow mortars called *metates* many miles from any source of the supply of such stone. They were so heavy I could hardly lift them. It is hard to believe the Indians would use such stones unless transportation were easy, as it would have been by canoe.

I got my first tip on this country from an old-timer who had been there during World War I, buying horses for the French and English armies from Bill Brown, the "Horse King." William Walter Brown was one of the most colorful figures who controlled a range empire in the sagebrush country. It is estimated that at his peak he owned nearly forty thousand acres of land, ten thousand horses, and more than twice that many sheep.

Fort Rock

It is from this crescent-shaped ancient crater that the valley gets its name, and calling this rock a fort is appropriate. It is an isolated mass, approximately a third of a mile across, with several cliffs reaching two hundred feet in height. Its highest point is 325 feet above the plain. Fort Rock was used as a place of defense by warring Indians, and once aided in the preservation of an immigrant train. The pioneers had wandered from the trail when they discovered a band of hostiles were following them. Reaching Fort Rock ahead of the enemy they blocked the approach with wagons and successfully stood off their assailants.

About 1904, under the stimulus of the enlarged desert homestead act, and the talk of irrigation and dry farming, most of the land of Fort Rock Valley was filed on. The settlers pulled and burned the sage, and plowed the ground. As the best farming land was the higher ground, they naturally cleared the old camp sites. In a few years these desert homesteaders had all become discouraged and left. I first went into the valley in 1923, when not a soul was living there. The wells were dry and the houses were occupied by wood rats and big horned owls. There were few of the roads we could drive over because of the drifting sand; but when the valley was first settled, there was no drifting sand. The ground was covered with bunch and rye grass as well as sagebrush and greasewood.

The sand in most of the valley is coarse and does not blow away easily, hence few dunes are formed, as they are in the light sands of the upper Columbia. Now a few are forming from the fields of the settlers, where the plowing gave the wind such a good chance.

In the northeast corner of the valley near dry Fossil Lake is an enormous stretch of dunes about a mile wide and ten miles long. It is crawling easterly through an island of young pine timber. Much of this sand has come from the dry bed of Christmas Lake and the alkali flats about it. Christmas Lake got its name from someone's belief that it was the lake Captain John C. Fremont named. This was an error, as Fremont never saw this lake. His Christmas Lake was one of the chain of Warner Lakes far to the south.

When I first visited the valley there was a passable road running north and south along the west side, a road across the north; also a road around each side of Table Mountain, which came together northeast of the mountain. Then it ran northeasterly and east to Lake Post Office and beyond to Wagontire. Lake Post

These rocks are but a small part of those that were once on this old desert camp site. The largest object, a *metate*, shows the size of the stones the Indians took several miles out into the valley; they may have carried them in canoes part way. Though this site covered more than five acres, none of the stones in this picture was moved over fifty feet.

Fort Rock . . . An idea of its size can be had from the tiny speck on the left at the top, which is a forest lookout station. In the foreground are clumps of rye grass, which survives well in dry country. The stiff tops mark the clumps. This grass has saved the lives of many head of cattle and horses in winter, when they paw it out of the snow.

Office was the only occupied place, and it had the only water anywhere — from near Silver Lake to a well at an abandoned place thirty miles east of a lake called Butte.

Nothing is found on the low ground, which is the old lake beds, except an occasional stray article that some settler or sheepherder might have dropped.

I have heard that an immense amount of relics was taken out of Fort Rock Valley by the settlers, particularly mortars, pestles, and other fine rocks, and the larger chipped pieces. I found what appeared to be the culls of collections thrown out at many abandoned cabins. One of the post offices in the valley was even called "Arrow." It was northeast of Silver Lake but was abandoned when the homesteaders left.

In April 1927, I furnished information and pictures to an *Oregonian* feature writer, who was required to give the location in his two articles. In the following May, R. H. Miller, a fellow-collector, to whom I had also given the information, visited the valley to find nine automobiles of relic hunters there ahead of him. Since that time, hundreds of people have gone there to collect. At Silver Lake, arrowheads were sold to tourists. There are still many large village sites not yet blown out, which some day may produce many relics, but the hunting will never be very good again. Relics will be picked up as fast as they come to light.

Through the valley, along the three or four main roads, I found the ground quite cleared of relics, but back away from them, in some isolated places, the blown-out fields seemed not to have been touched since the settlers left. Now, enthusiastic arrowhead hunters have dreams. A few of these spots were where such dreams come true. The richest place I found was less than a half acre in area. It had been blown out enough to expose most of the relics. They were not deeply covered—from a few inches to a foot, in most cases. From this small site I took over four hundred keepable chipped artifacts, consisting of arrowheads, spearheads, knives, drills, scrapers, and other shapes. I also took four packsack loads of rocks. All this had to be carried some three miles to the car. I left plenty. I found several other places that were not so rich, but quite rich enough to satisfy anyone.

From this trip of about ten days I came home with more than fifteen hundred chipped specimens and a thousand pounds of rock. I didn't see any article of personal adornment in this country.

I do not believe that the relics of this valley were left by the Snake Indians or that stones the size of some I found were carried by them twenty miles across country. The chipped work is the best I have seen anywhere in the desert country. Almost all is of obsidian but sometimes a piece is found of chalcedony or jasper. All are of valley workmanship. The most outstanding feature of the relics discovered here is the *mano*. This same grinding stone is found in the cliff dwellings and was given the name there—from the Spanish word for hand. The stones are from three to six inches long, three to four inches wide, and from a half inch to two inches thick. Considerable work was devoted to the making of one. When I first hunted in Fort Rock Valley I could have filled a truck with them. There are still quite a few left. I have not found this implement elsewhere in the desert country.

The Klamaths have a similar piece but it has one or two projections, presumably as a hand-hold, like the humps of a camel. A peculiar pestle, from eight to twelve inches long and two to four inches in diameter, was also quite common. Some of these were double-ended, resembling a hand grenade. While the center of the civilization that left these relics was Fort Rock Valley, it spread south over Silver Lake and westerly over Paulina Marsh. Who these Indians were, I do not attempt to say, but not Snakes, I believe, and not Klamaths.

I have never found a burial place, so cannot tell what form they took. The two or three bone pieces I have picked up were burned or partly petrified and thus were preserved. All signs of house sites have disappeared. A few graves have been found about Silver Lake, but they are plainly those of modern Snakes or other later Indians. I do not attempt to say who these valley Indians were or what became of them. I cannot tell whether the country was abandoned at the time it dried up last, or whether is was a long time before, during some other dry cycle. Where the wind and rain have cut some of those sharp ridges, Indian rocks are exposed at a depth of several feet. It would seem that the land was occupied before the ridges were built to these full heights. It is hard to see how the ridges could grow except when the lake beds were dry and their sand could be blown about. It would appear that the Indians had weathered one dry cycle at least.

The Klamath Indians were found by the first whites occupying the large marsh about fifty miles to the southwest of Fort Rock Valley. One might think that the Fort Rock Valley Indians merely retired to that part of the country when their own region dried up. Yet the Klamath Indians were living in houses placed on stilts in the water, and the valley Indians lived on high ground. Also, the implements of the Klamaths are very different. These include many fine mortars with flat bottoms for standing on level ground or floors. The grinding was done by pounding. The Fort Rock Valley Indians used but few pounding mortars, and most of these had sharp bottoms for jabbing into the sand. Mainly their grinding was done in shallow mortars or *metates*, or by rubbing. The whole setup of the Klamaths removes, from my mind at least, any thought that they may be the successors of the tribes of Fort Rock Valley.

And are the Calapooias their successors? I don't think so. The Calapooia Indians occupied the territory to the northwest of Fort Rock Valley, across the Cascade Mountains in the Willamette Valley. Their lands roughly extended from Oregon City, southerly to the Umpqua Indians near Roseburg. They also held the Tualatin Plains west and north of Portland. They were separated from the Chinooks on the Willamette and the Columbia by a ridge of hills that parallels the rivers.

At an old Calapooia camp site, about ten miles northwest of Portland, I found two types of small stone artifacts, exact duplicates of which I had picked up from the old sites of Fort Rock Valley. It all looked somewhat suspicious, but—to examine another side of it—I have found no *manos* in Calapooia territory. In Fort Rock Valley there were thousands of them. Would the use of them have been dropped just because the tribe crossed into another kind of country? The Fort Rock chipping was of the best, their arrowheads being of fine, perfect shapes. The Calapooia work was the worst I know of, their arrowheads being lopsided and roughly made. I see no reason for a tribe to lose its artistic sense or its ability to do fine workmanship.

I have noted in the writings of some of those making explorations among the cliff dwellers of Arizona and New Mexico the existence of a legend (apparently common to descendants of the cliff dwellers) which tells that their people came from the north and a land of many lakes. The cliff dwellers have now been proved to be about seven to eight hundred years old. The relics of Fort Rock greatly resemble those found in the cliff dwellings. The *manos* are exactly alike. Some years ago a picture was taken of about eight arrow points in a grave dug out down there. These were of unusual shapes, but I can duplicate every one of them from my Fort Rock collection. There are other similarities I could mention, but I am not trying to prove anything. I am just setting forth an idea.

Painted Hills

No photograph in black and white can properly show these colorful hills. One should see them just after a rain when the brilliant strata of red, green, and yellow are at their best. This picture was taken near the Bridge Creek Road between Mitchell and Burnt Ranch. There is a sign board on the road directing one to them. These are but one of the many interesting features of the John Day country in Central Oregon.

Chief Paulina

In Central Oregon a post office, a mountain, a lake, a marsh, a creek, a valley — and perhaps something I have missed — are named for this murderous old Snake Indian chief. He was, perhaps, the most dangerous of the several Snake chiefs whose bands roamed the southeast quarter of Oregon and beyond.

It is said that when he posed for this picture he didn't know what the camera was. He thought it might be some kind of gun. He knew he had plenty coming to him from the whites and he "suspicioned" he might be about ready to get some of it; so when they said, "hold still," he instinctively closed his eyes and put his hand over his heart. I must admit the old rascal was "going to take his medicine graceful." The picture was taken at Fort Klam ath sometime in the early 1860s, when Paulina was there under safe conduct to talk about him and his band going to the reservation.

Paulina was killed by Howard Maupin–for whom the town of Maupin was named–when he caught Paulina gorging on a beef he had killed. When Paulina found he had a fatal wound, he drove his knife deep into the ground until he broke the blade. It was an everlasting disgrace for an Indian to be scalped with his own knife. A chief named Ochoco succeeded him and in a few years made peace and moved with his band to the upper part of Sprague River on the Klamath Reservation, where they have since lived peacefully.

Fort Rock Cave.

Sandals such as this one from Oregon's interior desert country have been dated at nine thousand years by the "Carbon 14" method.

Part Three

THE AGE OF RELICS

I HAVE HEARD IT CLAIMED THAT CERTAIN CRUDE CHIPPED PIECES are very old because they were made before Indians had become advanced in the art of making them. There is nothing to this. When you have in hand about a thousand chipped pieces of all kinds to sort out and study, you soon dismiss any idea of crude ones meaning age. The rough ones are as good as the Indians cared to make them. Some Indians were no doubt better workmen than others, taking more pride in their work—or they were not as lazy as some others.

The purpose for which an arrow was to be used would influence its making. Extra-well-made scrapers, drills, or knives were probably valued possessions and, as such, were not carelessly kept; whereas pieces designed for a rough use might have been hurriedly made, and no better than the purpose required.

Large numbers of crude pieces are found that are not complete, though they appear at a glance to be so. Most of these pieces had, at one time, a short punching or gouging point, and were made for the use of this point. The point, however, was delicate in comparison to the weight of the whole piece; therefore it was more easily broken. In contrast to the delicate point, the handle end of such pieces was usually roughly shaped for convenience in holding. Some of them were real combination implements. It is these pieces, found broken or separated, that make up the majority of the crude implements so often considered old. They are found on the camp sites under the same conditions as the so-called good pieces, but few collectors know what they are.

Patina or surface texture on stone pieces means very little as it varies with the mineral content of the soil. I have found it on stones long underground, but not on those that have lain long on the surface. It no doubt takes time to form this age-mellowed or age-incrusted surface, but a hundred years would be considered old from this standpoint. In the desert country I have often found obsidian pieces with one side incrusted with a white substance, and I have spent some time figuring out a way to remove it. Several acids I tried had no effect whatever. I finally removed it with lye. My method was to put the pieces into a granite-ware or crockery vessel and cover it with a solution of about a heaping tablespoon of household lye to a quart of water. I slowly brought this to a boil, then kept it hot for about fifteen minutes. This softened the white coating so that it could be scraped off easily. When using this method, remember that obsidian is a form of glass and may break if dropped into hot water; also that this method is to be used only with obsidian. If it is used on some other stone, it will fog it and destroy the beauty of the piece.

In some situations the nature of the ground will give an indication of age. I know of relics that have come from under trees that were more than a hundred years old. As a camp site in the moist western region will generally seed itself almost as soon as it is abandoned, we can feel certain that the site had been abandoned but a short time when the trees started to grow. The relics found there would be at least as old as the tree.

Relics have been found at varying depths in places back from the rivers. Much that we know of them, though, is just hearsay. If positive information could be had of the many reports we hear about, perhaps something definite could be determined. Such deep finds are usually made by workmen digging wells; or they are located on other construction work. These workmen seldom take any interest in the scientific value of a find until someone starts a little excitement about it. Then they like to make the story good, so the pestle found on the dump comes from the bottom of the well. It is, however, from casual finds of this nature that we are going to get our evidence of depth—unless we can watch some of the deeper construction projects.

If an ordinary man of high education, but without a reputation as an authority on something or other, makes a find, he will get no further with it than the laborer who wants to make the story good. It would seem that the only way we can get evidence that is to bear weight is to take some husky workers to a likely spot and put some reputable men of science to watch them and each other. A similar technique has been used, with excellent results, by a number of groups, including the Oregon Archaeological Society, the University of Washington, and the University of Oregon.

I appreciate the fact that, when a find is made, it takes a person of some knowledge to determine the real status of the location: river changes, landslides, and workers all enter into it. Yet one can fully sympathize with any honest man who makes an interesting find and cannot get a hearing from anyone who bears weight. I have in mind an experience of my own some years ago. Snake authorities tell us that a mother snake never swallows her young to protect them, yet the following occurred:

I was fishing on a small stream near Portland, when I was attracted by four snakes of five or six inches in length that came out of some tall weeds onto the short, cattle-cropped grass within five feet of me. The snakes were abreast, four or five inches apart, doing lots of wiggling, but making little headway. Their actions and the fact that they were traveling abreast were both unnatural behavior for little snakes, so I watched them closely.

Slowly following, about two feet behind them, appeared the old snake. She was brownish gray in color, about twenty-two inches in length, and of that species of garter snake that we laymen generally call water snake. She brought her entire length into the open space before noticing the quiet fisherman, then she paused for a moment or two. Making a little sound, she lowered her head and opened her mouth. At her signal, the playful little snakes whirled about and streaked back to her and down her throat. Some had to wait for the others to get in. They passed down into her to the halfway point, or perhaps just a little farther. All four must have gathered at the same spot, because they caused a noticeable enlargement of her body at that point. The old snake remained perfectly still for about half a minute, with her head up a couple of inches. Then, after making a slight movement of her body, she lowered her head, and the little ones came out head first and struck out again in the same lively fashion as they had before she called them in off the grass.

I would like to agree with the authorities and say that there is no species of snake that swallows its young for protection—yet I saw it happen. This story has been told in all sincerity to men presumed to be authorities on snakes. From one I got the suggestion to produce the snake. Another asked, "What did you have on your hip that day?"

The point is that when a "find" is discovered in some isolated spot by an individual, it is exceedingly difficult for that person to establish its authenticity. On the other hand, it is very unfortunate when a naturalist of deservingly high reputation makes a mistake in stating something to be a fact that is not. Local professors and teachers repeat the mistake, using him as the authority; and the mistaken belief gets so firmly established that it is hard to upset. But I *saw* the snake swallow its young and am perfectly willing to go upon the stand to swear that I saw this happen; and the opposition may produce as many honest and learned witnesses as it likes to swear that they have never seen such a thing.

Some years ago, my friend R. H. Miller—one of the best and most persistent hunters of relics—saw a stone projecting from the river bank above Vancouver, Washington. In digging it out, he discovered a cache of forty-four perforated fishing sinkers. At this point the bank was about sixteen feet high and these sinkers were at the bottom. The bank had been cutting slowly away for as long as white men could remember. The deposit was not sediment in the true sense of the word, but a mixture of sand and clay such as is common along the lower Columbia River. These rocks must have been there a long time while that bank filled out and then cut back again. How long this had been going on I don't know, but I would feel safe in guessing at least two hundred years, whereas it might easily have been two thousand years.

It has been suggested—and to a small extent studied—that the higher benches of the Columbia near Celilo might solve the question of ancient occupancy. Personally, I have not found any convincing evidence along this line. Relics have been found on all these high benches, and no doubt Indians were living along the river when it was somewhat higher than it is at present, but I don't think they were there when the water level was at those high benches. In all probability, Celilo became a good fishing place only after the fault occurred that made the falls. The relics of these high benches are no different from those found along the present banks—now under the waters of Lake Celilo.

The first whites found a condition of peace among the Indians here; that is, many different tribes came here to fish, and they were seemingly in harmony. In the course of ages, however, the area may have passed through all kinds of conditions; and it is not unreasonable to assume that—in a place so long used by so many people and under such diverse conditions of peace and war —all the level ground anywhere about would at some time have been used as camp sites.

Poor Indians arriving before the salmon run started might have moved to these benches for the varieties of roots that grew there. Troublesome times might have caused groups of Indians to camp where they would be the most protected. Heavy implements might have been buried to hide them when a temporary absence was contemplated; and, through the adversities of life, the owners might never have returned. Because many different kinds of burials were practiced by the Indians living here, or by those who made the annual pilgrimage for fish, it is only natural that all this soil would be rich in relics of all ages. However, the high benches have produced little compared with the present banks.

Fountain Bar furnished me with a good study of the back benches of the river. This piece of river was, in my opinion, next to that of Celilo, the most heavily populated. Investigation has convinced me that the majority of Indian villages were along the river near places where the salmon in their upstream flow passed close to the bank. It is possible that, when the river was at a higher level, the places where I once found village sites were not fishing places at all. Such may have been the case at Fountain

Bar. However, here the river runs close to bedrock, and there has been little change in the last thousand years. With the completion of the John Day Dam, Fountain Bar will have gone the way of other famous Indian sites like Celilo Falls and Wishram.

For over half its two-mile length, Fountain Bar is in two benches, separated by a cliff about fifty feet high. The upper level is not as convenient as a living place, since it is farther from the water and from driftwood fuel. The fact that the greater part of both levels had been blown out to bedrock gave me a good chance to study them. The upper level showed almost nothing, but I did find a few chipped pieces, several short-occupancy camp sites, and some spots I took to be cremation pits. Some burial places had also been blown out here. The lower bar for its entire length was rich in relics, and large collections have been made from it. It seems clear that, before the river cut its present channel, the higher bar was at the bank, and it was not used as a camp site. Apparently the Indians used that bar only after the lower level was cut. I believe that such overall observations as these give insight as to the authentic age of camp sites and relics.

Petroglyphs—of which there are many along the river—show nothing of a period beyond a few hundred years at the very most. Largely because of weathering, it is difficult to determine the older of two groups of petroglyphs. Carvings of horses are sometimes found, and in some cases they were made over older carvings, but the horse carvings look as old as the earlier ones. All are subject to the winds and frost, and many of them to the annual floods. The winds carry much sand, and no petroglyph is going to look new for any great length of time, unless it is in a very protected place. In fact, the majority of them all look too nearly alike in age to differentiate among them.

Evidence of age has come, and will, I believe, continue to come from the caves of the interior desert country. A different culture may be unearthed there. That dry, alkaline soil would protect objects that would quickly disappear in the rainy section. Here in the desert valley, the greatest sign of age is seen in the large amount of relics, and in their general distribution, especially the many that turn up in unlikely places. For example, it must have taken considerable time to have discovered obsidian and so generally to have distributed it; some of it is found on almost every Indian camp site in Oregon. It also took time for so many different tribes to have arrived here, to have fought it out with their predecessors—if any—and to have become settled in the different territories.

Relics obviously made with the white man's tools are generally more recent than those made without them. But depth of the relics, especially in relation to geology of the area, is a more important clue, save for certain blown-out areas. Scientists in recent years have excavated to depths of thirty feet and over, deep into earth strata of the ice age, to find evidences of civilizations up to eleven thousand years old, right here in the Northwest. This dating is done by the "carbon 14" method, which at the present time is considered to be the most exact method of establishing age.

The theory behind this method is this: Carbon 14 is an unstable isotope of carbon with an atomic weight of 14. It is formed in the atmosphere at a constant rate through the bombardment of nitrogen atoms by cosmic rays. All living matter absorbs carbon 14 in the same definite proportion until death, when no more is absorbed to replace the carbon 14 which continues to break down even after death. A kind of geiger counter is used to determine the amount of carbon 14 left in the relic; the amount left indicates the age. The method works only on organic material.

If the Pacific Northwest Indians came from Asia—which is the established belief now—they must have been here a long time for the environmental conditions to have caused their skins to turn red. I personally think that they have occupied this territory since the salmon began their great runs in our rivers, and since geologic changes left a land suitable for wappato and camas to grow in such abundance. Count all these factors in years, if you can.

Double paint-mortar.

Part Four

TYPES OF RELICS

RELICS CAN GENERALLY BE DIVIDED INTO THREE LARGE GROUPS: utility, personal adornment, and unclassified pieces. Implements of utility can then be separated into various classes according to the use for which they were intended. Some interesting pieces are but the tools with which other implements were made. Some, made for a special purpose, might have been used for still other purposes for which they were later found handy. I am classifying them here according to the purpose for which they were originally intended. Other collectors might use a different system of classification, and both of us might be right.

It is in the types of these classes that the obscurity lies for most student collectors. Such pieces which might be classed as fishing weights would include many forms. The Indians had about twenty different ways of taking fish. Net and line sinkers are of many forms: banded gravel with one or several bands; flat perforated stones from two to ten inches across, with the hole bored anywhere from the center to an end; flat gravel broken into rectangular shapes from two by four to three by six inches; flat gravel stones from one to six inches across and notched in one, two, or four sides. These and others I classify as types of fishing weights.

Digging stones, in the simplified form, consist of a gravel stone broken into two pieces so as to give the pieces a beveled edge. Another form is a stone, say seven inches in length, chipped on one side to a more or less long beveled digging edge. A more advanced form is like this last one, but the face may be concave and polished. Again it may, at the hand-hold end, have grooves cut for the thumb and the fingers. In its highest form it may be a work of art, polished over-all and beautifully shaped somewhat

like a bricklayer's trowel. One could call each of these a different type or just one type to differentiate them from flat, shovel-
shaped diggers of laminated basalt or of sedimentary rock. I call
them different types.

In proportion to the utility objects, the personal adornment
and unclassified objects are rare. Personal adornment objects of
stone include pendants of ornamental pieces of flat slate and
other stone. Some of these are chipped and some are polished.
Nose and ear pieces are comparatively rare, but stone beads of
many sizes and shapes have been found in abundance, especially
at a few locations along the rivers. Occasionally one will see for
sale, in some curio or art shop, beautiful little chipped articles
such as tomahawks, birds, stars, and such. I regret that these
are being sold as old Indian pieces. Just try to find them on the
old camp sites. They are to the hunter of Indian relics what the
imitations of old stamps made in Japan or Switzerland are to the
stamp collector. One curio dealer offered to have made for me
any fancy shape for which I drew a model.

Regarding the stone relics of unknown purpose—these might
have been produced to pass away the time. The natural form of
a stone might have suggested a shape to the maker, and only one
such shape might be found. An artistic urge in a workman could
have found its outlet in such a piece. Or, the object might have
had some religious or ceremonial significance.

Identification of Relics

When a beginner finds an obscure stone piece, there are two
things that he should realize. The first of these is that any kind
of Indian implement or object may be found highly developed,
even to a point worthy of being called a work of art. Indians
did not confine their artistic efforts to the better pieces such as
mortars, pestles, or paint cups; rather, they covered the entire
field from the grinding tools—with which other implements were
made—up to the finest mortars. The second thing to realize is
that implements were often developed to such a high point that
today it is difficult to determine their original use or purpose.
This elaboration was sometimes carried so far that the practical
use was greatly reduced.

144

It is quite evident that most of the Indians' work could have been done with suitable, naturally shaped stones, or with selected forms which would have required little work to make them useful. But the desire to possess something to treasure, the desire to be better, or to be different from a neighbor, was a strong factor in inducing them to spend time and energy in the elaboration of the pieces. Some implements were, of course, greatly improved because of the work put into them.

It is also well to remember that the material at hand was generally used for making many of the practical implements. Along the lower and sandy parts of the Columbia, gravel could be had from the river banks, hence most digging and splitting tools were made from it. A few miles eastward, however, basalt cliffs came down close to the camp grounds. Here, tools were frequently made by roughly chipping pieces of this stone. In certain parts of the John Day country, laminated sedimentary rock was so used. Such things as these must be taken into consideration in any serious study of the implements.

It is in these chipped pieces that there is more difficulty in separating the types. They can easily be divided into cutting or scraping edges, drilling or punching points, and gouging ends; but each of these types must have had a purpose. It must have been used in some special work or upon a certain kind of object, and we don't have this information—nor do we think anyone else has, or will find it, at this late day. We could infer that the heavier or stronger implements were used on larger objects, but in this we might be mistaken.

Perhaps it would be better to try to determine what material the chipped pieces were used upon: wood, bone, horn, or stone. Some of these pieces, such as the duckbill scraper, are found the world over. These different peoples must have had the same purpose in view in making them. The obscurity, however, does not lie in the number of types—though there are more of these than most collectors know—but rather in the apparent overlapping of the uses. That is, it is difficult to see why, with some of them, one would not have served the need as well as another. Perhaps two of them were used for the same purpose, but one was shaped differently to serve as the fastening of a handle. We don't know.

Combination Types

In discussing the age of relics I mentioned that some pieces were used in combination: one end might be a drill, and the other, the handle-end, a cutting or scraping edge. Several such combinations occur. A great many pieces have a punching point on the end or side, and the body is shaped like a rough knife or even like a spear point. When the delicate point is broken off, the body becomes an obscure object, often considered to be a rough arrowhead, if small; or a knife, if large. It is well to examine such pieces carefully to see if they show where points have been.

It is interesting to note that some types are found in certain localities but not in others where it is apparent there would have been no use for them. For example, on the coast I found a little chipped implement used in opening clams or mussels that is not found in the desert country. This piece varies from one to seven inches in length. I determine types in these small objects by trying to find a large number shaped just alike. Then if they are new to me, I feel I have made a small discovery. Some of these types I have shown to other collectors who have later located many of them.

Someone has said that the man who got the keenest enjoyment out of life was the naturalist with a leg-hold on a new species of grasshopper. I have had a bit of this feeling in discovering some new types of chipped pieces. Since several hundred of them are necessary for any worthwhile study, I have made a practice of bringing home every piece I found that had the Indian mark on it. Then, when I had accumulated about a bushel of them, I went to work. Some of the types of implements I discovered are included here.

Except for arrow points, mortars and pestles are probably the most well known of all the artifacts.

Mortars and Pestles

Pestles from the Seaman Collection.

At the extreme right of the above photograph, on the middle line you see a rather long pestle, the upper end of which comes to a sharp edge. It had a double use, as a grinding pestle and as a wood-splitting tool. On this same middle line, and next to the extreme right, is a long, quite slender pestle. This was used for packing dried salmon into deep baskets.

The use of the mortar and pestle for grinding and pulverizing dates back to prehistoric times when they were employed mainly for making flour. The mortar is generally shaped like a basin or vase and is found in a number of materials, the Indians often shaping them of wood. Though the pestles were of many shapes and sizes, they are usually elongated, club-shaped tools, sometimes with a knob at one or both ends.

Pestles were among the commonest stone implements because

nearly all preserved Indian foods were dried and were therefore hard. The Indian method of cooking—by dropping hot rocks into a wooden bowl or water-tight basket — was naturally crude and slow. Since with this method the food had to be cooked liquid, soup was commonly served; and hard foods, like dried salmon, were ground or pounded with mortar and pestle for the best and the quickest cooking. Hence, these implements were on hand at all campfires.

"Kitchen Tables"

Pestles were used not only for grinding in mortars but also for hammering on their "kitchen tables": large flat stones that served in place of mortars. I have found these flat stones on the sites of many old camps along the Columbia. They were, roughly, sixteen to twenty inches square, and six to seven inches thick. If the ground on which they rested was uneven, they were leveled up with small flat stones. In the center of the stone there was generally found a depression from one-fourth to one-half inch deep, depending upon how much work had been done on it. About Celilo, where there were many permanent villages, this stone was replaced by a similar large stone that was cut like a mortar and was about four inches deep. Around Tule Lake, the Indians, probably Modocs, used similar large stones, but with two or three small mortars of varying depth ground into them.

In case you wonder why an Indian woman would go to all the work to shape a fine pestle when she could walk out onto almost any sand bar and pick up a natural stone that would do the job as well as the fanciest pestle—the answer is simple. We must remember that the Indians had few things they could accumulate for wealth or display, so the woman would probably be proud, when guests came, to bring forth a fine pestle with which to pound the dried salmon. She might produce it naturally, just as if it were the only kind she ever used.

Some of the pestles were as much as twenty inches in length and less than three inches in their greatest diameter. These were used for packing dried salmon into deep baskets; and they are a good example of an elaborate implement made for a short-time use. They were used only in the fishing season and did work that could have been done as well, and in most cases was done, with a simple wooden rammer. The handy pestle was also one of those implements that served a number of purposes. About the camp, a pestle often took the place of a hammer in the modern home, since it was used for such general purposes as cracking nuts or driving stakes into the ground.

Paint and medicine mortars.

The bottom row in the above picture shows mortars used for grinding, mixing, or holding face paints, while the larger mortars on the top row—except for the far-right piece—are said to have been used to hold medicines. The upper right stone is a rare type, and there has been considerable speculation as to its use. My own opinion is that it is an end sinker on a net because it shows wear on the bottom end and in the same place where a sinker would normally show wear. The float above it would keep it bouncing up and down on the sand or stone of the river bottoms.

Mortars, pestles, and *metates*.

This picture, a part of the Marshall-Seaman collection, shows some desert-country mortars and pestles. The large mortar at the right was found on the west bank of Lake Abert and has the flat bottom customarily found where the ground is level and hard.

The large chipped mortar in the center, the smaller mortar just above it, and the still smaller mortar just to the right of it all show the rounded or sharp bottoms used in the sandy country. The heavy mortar on the stool at the left came from the extreme south end of Goose Lake. It is peculiar in the fact that the hole is only four inches wide, but over ten inches deep.

On the floor are shown two large, shallow mortars called *metates*, a Spanish word. These were once very common in Fort Rock Valley, but they are now scarce. In the *metate* to the left is a heavy double-ended pestle common to the valley. Pestles to be used as hammers and slender ones for grinding in mortars were quite rare in this area.

The *metates, manos* (hand stones for grinding), the chipped work, the scarcity of personal adornment pieces, and the fact that I have found no graves there—all these observations have led me to believe that the Fort Rock people belonged to the Shoshone race.

Mano is from the Spanish word meaning hand—an appropriate name for these hand stones for grinding. I have found them only in Fort Rock Valley, though I understand they are to be seen in the cliff dwellings of Arizona and New Mexico. The larger ones are about six inches in length. They are from one-half to one and one-half inches in length; and from one-half to one and one-half inches thick. Some have but one working face, while others have two.

Manos

The faces on many of these grinding stones are perfect planes. On others they are slightly convex, leading one to believe that some may have been used on a *metate*. If they had been, the face would have become convex as *metates* are concave. The plane faces would suggest the use of one against another; that is, one would be held in each hand in a basket. I believe this because I have found many in pairs in isolated places. They were very plentiful in Fort Rock Valley when I first went there.

The center stone with horns on it is a common type of the Klamath Indians. I have never found any like it in Fort Rock Valley.

Mortars and Bowls

Frank Wilke Collection
Stone mortar from the Atlatl Valley site, on the Washington shore west of
Wakemap Mound.

The following pictures illustrate how much work was sometimes put in on Columbia River mortars. The upper two are the
two sides of the same bowl, but they were chalked in to show the
varying design. The lower one, found on the Bead Patch, was
photographed "natural." It still retained traces of the red and
green paint with which it had been covered. It was probably
used by a medicine man in his ceremonies. A number of bowls
roughly made of lava rock were found, including several that
were dug out of the solid base rock of the camp site.

Carved Bowl—chalked in.

Carved Bowl—"natural."

Fancy paint cup or mortar.

Carved paint mortar.

Rubbing, Grinding, and Polishing Stones

On camp sites many stones are found for rubbing leather, cutting on wood, and for grinding and polishing stones. Such stones were of the utmost importance in Indian work, but they seem to get little attention in most collections. These stones appear in a number of different materials including sandstone and scoriac lava. It is natural that stones of different texture would have been used. Coarse, but fast, cutting on wood could be done best with scoriac lava, whereas bone and horn would require a finer-grained cutting material. Natural, smooth stones are often found; and they were, perhaps, very suitable for such purposes as rubbing tanned buckskin while it was drying. On the other hand, a rough grain would have been injurious.

Rubbing, grinding, and polishing stones.

Occasionally one of these stones, because of its excellent shape, became an Indian's most valued tool; perhaps it did a particularly good job for some regular work such as rubbing hair off hides. These stones are seldom picked up by relic hunters unless some mark of the Indian is upon them, such as a groove to fit some object being worked upon.

Mauls, Wedges, and Wood Splitters

Many of the multi-purpose tools of the Northwest Indians were the same as those that have been used from prehistoric times throughout the world. Natives here also had their wedges and mauls, their hammers and their knives and chisels. Most of these were stone, though many of the wedges for wood splitting were fashioned from elkhorn or wood. The cutting edges for the stone tools were generally flaked and chipped or "pecked"; that is, they were struck with sharp, rapid blows until they reached the shape the workman desired; then they were ground and polished.

Mauls and hammers, from hand-sized stones to highly ornamented hammerheads, were among the earliest and most common tools. Thousands of simple stones that were used as implements have gone unnoticed, but they can be identified by the signs of use. Characteristic of the Northwest tribes were the bottle-shaped mauls, but there were some variations.

Stone maul found on Lady Island, near Camas.

156

Some of the so-called hammerheads might have been anchors or banded fishing weights. A number of the sinkers are quite elaborate; these were the ones often used as the end sinker on a net. They were believed to charm the salmon into the net. If a net tore loose and lodged downstream, these sinkers would also serve to mark the ownership of the net.

Sinkers, mauls, and wedges.

In this picture, banded fishing sinkers form the top and bottom rows. The three club-shaped pieces are stone wood-splitting mauls. Near the center are elkhorn wedges and a piece of horn from which a wedge was made.

With infinite labor, the Indians used their elkhorn wedges, their mauls and adze blades, and their elkhorn or beaver-teeth chisels to split the boards from giant logs to build their houses.

With these primitive tools they shaped the wood to construct their canoes, and with their wedges and splitters they cut their firewood. Where there were slaves, they, of course, did much of the heavy work.

Preparing Firewood

One would naturally suppose that, in a timbered country such as the lower Columbia section, an Indian would never need to split firewood. This, however, was not the case. Whenever a camp remained for a time in one place, the wood on the ground, or in the river drifts, soon became scarce. It was then necessary or economical to split the larger pieces. The Indians started the split with elkhorn or wooden wedges driven in with mauls like the three shown in the illustration. This operation was followed up with wood-splitters. The mauls are self-explanatory when you have them in hand. The hand-holds are well cut in. The working faces show the wear; in fact, so much is worn off some of them that they could not have been used only on horn or wood. Stones found about the campfires show that stone wedges were used when Indians could find naturally shaped stones suitable for the purpose. Stone splitting tools were not struck or driven with mauls. Some pioneer writings tell of Indians splitting wood with elkhorn wedges and green, bottle-shaped mauls. The shortest maul shown here is of that tough, green rock. It is somewhat bottle-shaped.

Today, when we split heavy pieces such as cordwood, we use splinter bars or perhaps peavies to tear apart cross splinters. The stone "wood-splitters" of the Indians were their tool for the same purpose. They were used for any splitting that was done and were one of the principal tools used in canoe making. They were often elaborate and ranged from six to fourteen inches in length. Natural rock substitutes can be found on some camp sites, but they are seldom noticed. I have found the splitters on both sides of the Columbia, but have never seen evidence that they were used with a handle. The splitters shown here are all polished pieces.

Diggers

The prehistoric digging stick was about the simplest and most common of the primitive tools. Because it was often merely a sharpened stick, it soon rotted away. Still it is dramatic to consider that this modest implement evolved into some of mankind's most useful tools. From it came the spades and shovels, the hoes and picks, the plows and harrows, and eventually the steam shovels and bulldozers.

Digging stones and wood-splitters.

In the center row of this picture are shown wood-splitting tools, with a side view of two of them to show the sharp edge. Digging stones are shown in the top and bottom rows. On each side of the bottom line are diggers made of spalls.

Though the digging sticks were highly perishable, the stone diggers were not, and these are found in great number, but most often away from regular camp sites. They were apparently left or lost where roots were being dug. As mentioned earlier, the simplest type of stone digger was made by breaking a flat stone to give a beveled edge. A better digger was made by chipping the beveled edge to a longer digging edge. The next advance was made from a stone carefully selected for a good hand-hold and chipped to a long and pointed edge. Then came the digger with a polished edge and grooves cut for the thumb and fingers. The finest of the diggers are near to being works of art; they have small handles and are shaped like sugar scoops. This sequence of improvement or elaboration is found in almost all classes of Northwest Indian artifacts.

In the area of the rock cliffs about ten miles above Vancouver, Washington, I have found diggers made of sharpened spalls—chipped pieces from the cliffs; also some from the laminae, the flaked layers of rock. The latter are given a sharp digging edge by a cross seam.

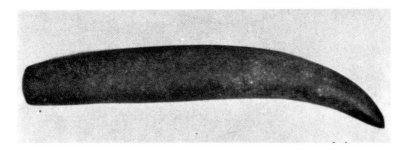

Stone tool for digging camas.

The camas digger shown here is about nine and a half inches long and beautifully made. It is a good illustration of a fancy treasure piece upon which a great amount of hard work has been done; a sharp stick would have done its work just as well. There is a little story that goes with this relic: One day at a Portland curio shop, where my friend Robert Miller used to visit, the proprietor showed him two so-called camas diggers that he had just received from California. Mr. Miller examined them with interest, as he had never seen any like them before. The very next day he was hunting along the north bank of the Columbia River, a few miles above Vancouver, and he found the one shown. I once found a half of one in Fort Rock Valley.

An eight-inch antler digging stick handle from Sauvies Island . . . some say that such a handle was made for a young girl when she first started to assist in gathering the family food; that she kept it all her lifetime, and that it was buried with her.

Basalt-slab digging tools—also likely used for removing bark and hollowing out canoes.

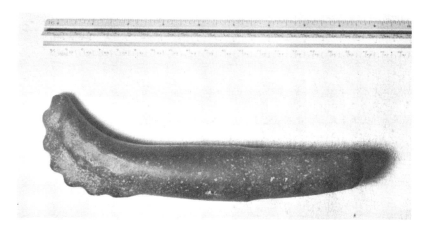

Stone artifact, probably a club.

Adzes

For Northwest Indians, the adze served as an axe, but it differed from an axe in having an arching blade set at right angles to the handle. Though the usual shape of the adze was that of

Monolithic adze blade. Some collectors call these "stone wedges."

an elbow, it was made in a variety of shapes according to the notions of the producer. To change the shape, it was only necessary to set the blade on the handle at a different degree or angle. Adzes with stone handles having a J-shape have been found along the southern Oregon coast. While northward, in the Puget Sound country, definitely U-shaped ones have been picked up. In length, the blades range from one to sixteen inches. Though sometimes used in the hand, the blades were more often attached to a handle to make an adze.

Adze blades.

Various materials were used for the blades, a common one being jadeite, a handsome, tough green stone that takes a high polish as well as a sharp edge. Jadeite is found in the North and along the Rogue River in southern Oregon. Whatever the material—stone, bone, or shell—the blades invariably were attached to the handle so that they could be drawn toward the worker who was making the stroke, giving him entire control of the tool. Adze "pocking marks" appear on many of the early Indian products of the Pacific Northwest, including totem poles and house planks. It would seem that the rippled appearance caused by the stroke of the adze was regarded as decorative, much as the adze-marked beams of ceilings were later.

Adze, blades, and flints.

At the top of this picture is a Columbia River adze. The line below shows four bits detached from the horn or bone end pieces that once held them. They have nicely polished cutting edges. Complete adzes are extremely rare, but the bits are not uncommon. The small objects on the third line are often mistaken for Indian work, but actually they are the flints from an old-time flintlock musket and are shown for the information of collectors who might be puzzled by them. The broken bit on the bottom line is from a blade of jadeite. The complete adze is the property of the Oregon Historical Society.

Adze blades made from jadeite. The Columbia River Indians had no regular axes; they used the adze in a wooden or bone handle.

Flintlock musket.

The flints were used on old flintlock muskets like this one, though there wasn't one on the gun when this picture was taken. Still you can see how they functioned. The two jaws of the hammer and the screw by which the jaws were closed or opened show plainly. The flint was put between the jaws and the screw tightened. When the trigger was pulled, the flint struck the steel standing in front of the hammer. This caused a spark to ignite the loose powder held in a cup at the base of the steel. Such a musket is now considered a crude weapon, but it brought death to many men and animals.

Saws, Knives, and Arrow Straighteners

Row 1: The two pieces shown here are saws made from thin spalls of basalt. This appears to be the most satisfactory Indian tool for cutting timber up to a couple of inches in diameter. The larger one is seven inches long. The cutting edges of both are rough and were made by alternately chipping one way and then the other. Looking down the edges, I found that they very much resemble our own saws. Both saws, alike except in size, were found about thirty miles apart. Others of basalt with this chipped edge are found in different shapes, but all are referred to as saws.

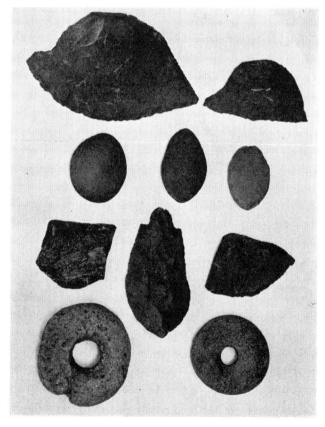

Saws, knives, and arrow straighteners.

Row 2: These three polished salmon cleavers were found near Celilo. They were made from spalls of basalt. Their average length is about three inches; the thickness, a fourth to a half inch at the center. Farther up the Columbia, I have found the same implement nicely chipped from handsome stone. Many are quite beautiful specimens.

Row 3: The two side pieces here are similar to the saws in line 1, but are of a much finer chipping. They were likely used for more finished work on wood. The use of the center piece is obscure; it has a sharp cutting edge on each side, and was used in a handle. The Indians tell me it was a cleaver for breaking or separating bones in large game.

Row 4: These are called doughnuts by collectors. This is an appropriate name, for they resemble them. They were used for taking little bends or kinks out of wooden arrows. The arrow was inserted in the hole and pressure was brought to bear on the bend. They seem to have been a stone favored by the Indians to make into an implement for show—and they certainly would not have worn out. These are of volcanic rock and measure three and a half by four inches in diameter, and about one inch in thickness.

Columbia River knives . . . The knife with the stem at the far left of the top row is extremely rare.

Columbia River knives.

Columbia River knife ground from slate.

Columbia River knives called "broad-horn" or "mule-ears."

Columbia River knives made from petrified wood.

Arrow-shaft Straighteners

Arrow shafts were made from many different kinds of wood, one of the best having been cedar. They were rounded and polished by means of "straighteners" or "smoothers" fashioned from some abrasive stone like pumice or sandstone. Often nicely shaped, like the ones on the facing page, they show the skill and pride of the maker.

These straighteners are frequently found in pairs, having been used that way. Because the center grooves do not touch when the stones are pressed together, by using pressure, the inserted shaft could be straightened and smoothed when pulled through the grooves. The type of straightener shown below was made of smooth, dense stone and is thought to have been heated and used with oil for straightening the shafts.

Arrow-shaft straighteners used while hot to take the kinks out of the shafts.

Arrow-shaft straighteners and smoothers of abrasive stone.

Atlatl Weights

A recent discovery by two eastern Oregon cave explorers, near Condon, Oregon, has proved that such flat-bottomed, banded stones as the one shown here are atlatl or throwing-stick weights. Their "find" in this arid region consisted of two throwing sticks, one of which still had the weight bound to it. One of these throwing sticks was about sixteen inches long and an inch and a half wide, with a groove down the center. At the base of the stick was a hollow area for seating the weight, which was fastened to the base with grass twine. The throwing stick without the weight was only twelve inches long; it could have been a child's throwing stick or one used for ceremonial purposes.

Atlatl weight.

The weight shown here is of quartzite gravel and highly polished; it must have been difficult to make from so hard a stone. The band about the river-form is at the center, like the one shown here, while the band about the desert-form is at the ends.

Though atlatls have been found with this type weight in place, there are some who believe this implement was a medicine man's measuring stone. They say that those seeking his assistance were required to cover the stone with whatever seed, bulb, or other article they were using to pay for the service. Feathers were tied in the grooves around the ends of the stones to make them look more ceremonious and also to make them cover a larger area. However, if they were these measuring stones, the Indian doctors must have required several sizes of stones in order to measure the different articles they might receive as pay.

Banded atlatl weight (above), and drilled atlatl weight (below) from The Dalles area.

Bark Breakers, Moccasin Lasts, and Gaming Stones

The two pieces at the upper right and upper left of this picture are forms for making moccasins, according to an old pioneer who often saw them used. The one at the extreme right is flat and could be used for either foot by simply turning it over. They were found on the camp sites of the Rogue River Indians of southern Oregon; they are not used on the Columbia, or very rarely so.

Bark breakers, moccasin lasts, and gaming stones.

The pointed or oval stones between the moccasin lasts were used as picks for breaking bark or knocking it off logs, or for tearing rotten logs and stumps to pieces for cedar roots or pitch wood. They range between five and seven inches in length and nearly all have a socket for the handle end. They are not rare yet, but they certainly are not plentiful. Like the digging stones, they are more often found away from the camp sites, where they were carelessly left or lost.

The disk-shaped stones, in groups of three on each side near the center, are of uncertain use. They are found only on Calapooia Indian camp sites. They are from three to five inches in diameter and from one and one-fourth to one and a half inches thick. Some are quite round, but others are somewhat oval. Had they been used in a game of rolling stones, they would have been cut or ground round. If they had been used as a grinding stone, they would have been worn round with use; the narrow edge is the working part. Being fine grained and hard, though, they would have been good grinding stones.

The sphere in the center of the bottom line is a cannon ball. The three spheres to the right and to the left of it are gaming stones used to roll at holes in the ground; perhaps they are the grandfathers of our modern golf ball. They are two and a half to four inches in diameter and are found on the Columbia River, the desert, and the Calapooia camp sites.

Stone balls or "gaming stones" such as these are found throughout the Northwest.

Atlatls and Breaking Stones

Row 1 shows different-sized atlatl weights. The center stone is four and one-half inches in length, two and one-half inches high, and two inches wide. All are of basalt or scoriac lava.

Atlatls and breaking stones.

The objects in *Row 2* are made of flat gravel stones from one-half to three-fourths of an inch thick, and are chipped to a beveled edge, some half way around, and others around the entire perimeter. These stones have had a variety of interpretations. It has been suggested that they were used as throwing stones, but it is hard to agree with this as some of them are quite small, only a little over an inch in diameter. For this reason they could hardly have been conceived as an effective weapon. Occasionally one is found that is nearly six inches across, but it would be difficult to hold to throw. Some believe that such stones were held in a split handle and were used as a hammer or breaking stone to reduce chipped work in its early stages. They are very plentiful on both the lower and the upper river, and one would expect

them to be plentiful, if they were used in making chipped articles. However, the fact that so many of these stones have been
found close to the water's edge—and also the fact that they are
rare on the camp sites—leads me to believe that they were used
in fishing or in scaling salmon. Archeologists call them cobble
choppers.

Row 3 shows two breaking stones of the desert country,
where they are plentiful on the camp sites and are the only suitable breaking stones found there. In the picture they appear flat,
but they are round and indicate use over the entire surface. They
are of tough basalt, and do not appear to have had a handle.

Slave Killers and Fire Makers

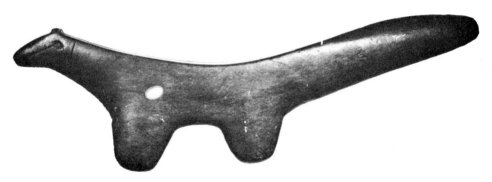

Mertie Stevens Collection
Slave killer from The Dalles. These bladed clubs are rare.

The center piece in this picture has been called a "slave killer" by some collectors, but to be complete it should have the handle-end extended to nearly twelve inches. I do not vouch for the claim that they were used in killing slaves, but this would not be contrary to Indian thought. There is good evidence of slaves being killed and of their being tied and placed in the houses of the dead so that they could go to the happy hunting grounds with their masters. Such objects as these are rare, but a few have been found along the Columbia.

Slave killer and fire makers.

At the right in this picture are two concave pieces that could have served several purposes: they could have been used at the fire end of a firestick to hold punk or pitch scrapings to help friction to start the fire; they could have been used at the upright end of a firestick as a protection for the hand; or they could have been used to hold the upper end of a bowstring drill.

At the left is a stone cube, the purpose of which is unknown. It came from a Calapooia Indian camp near Portland, and is the only one of the kind I have ever found. I would judge it to be a grinding or polishing stone intentionally worn into a cube shape.

War Club Heads

All the objects shown in this picture could have been used as weapons; but those on the top line—with the exception of the cener piece—could also have been diggers used with handles. The center piece is grooved for a handle; with a handle it would have been a wicked weapon or a poor specimen of an axe.

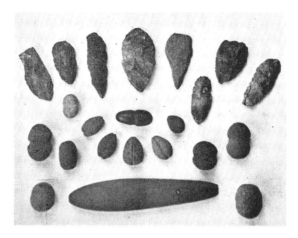

War club heads.

The banded gravel stones shown are the proper weight for war club heads. Some of them have a pit in the side to hold the end of a handle. Such stones could have been used for sinkers, but the ends are well rounded, and those on the larger stones that I know are sinkers do not have well-rounded ends. The rounded ends also make them unsuitable for camp-use hammers, which usually have flattened ends.

The pear-shaped plummets shown in this same picture have been controversial specimens for years, but judging from what I have been able to gather from the Indians and others, I believe they were used as fishing charms. The groove held bunches of feathers to make them ornamental and also a thong for suspending the charm over the water—from the end of a pole stuck into the sand. I doubt if we will ever find out if the Indians were entirely superstitious about these charms. They may have thought they excited the curiosity of the fish, so that they would come closer to the fisherman on the bank.

The long pestle-like stone at the bottom of the picture is an unusual piece about which nothing much is known. It is over three inches wide and little more than an inch thick. Its shape would be unsatisfactory for packing salmon, it shows no wear from use, its thinness would prevent its use as a maul to drive elkhorn wedges, and it could easily be broken. If it were intended as a weapon, one would expect a better hand-hold. It is too heavy to carry around on the warpath—though if a big Indian with that rock were chasing me down the creek bottom, it wouldn't take much argument to get me to agree that he was carrying a deadly weapon. I am led to believe that it comes as near to being a ceremonial stone as anything found in this territory.

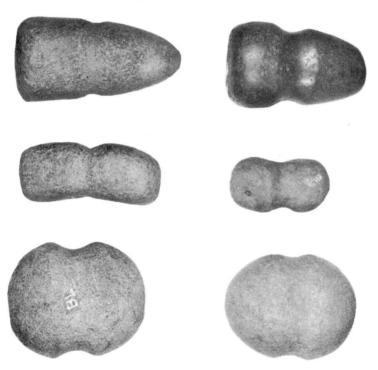

Stone war club heads. The two at the bottom could also be sinkers.

Fishing Sinkers

All the specimens in this picture are fishing rocks except the ones on the lower right and left, which are canoe anchors and were sometimes used on a net. Because the winds and current of the Columbia River often are very strong, it was sometimes necessary to put out a stern anchor to prevent the canoe from being thrown sideways against the rocks. This, of course, was in places where it was not convenient to pull the canoe up onto the land.

The small, flat gravel notched on each side is probably the commonest Indian fishing rock found along our rivers. The three oblong ones in the center are four to six inches in length and

Fishing sinkers.

three-fourths of an inch thick. Not much is known about the use of the different-sized stones. The large net sinkers we know about; it is the small ones that are puzzling. The latter are no longer familiar to the Indians of today; at least, I have had little success in finding anything out about them.

Stone Images

These stone figures are more plentiful along the lower river than they are east of the mountains, and it is very probable that this is because of the lack of cliffs suitable for carving. The artistic urge would find its outlet through these large gravel images.

Owl.

Frog.

I have never been able to learn of any religious significance attached to them. In fact, the Indians take them quite lightly. One called them just pictures. Another said they sometimes set them up in camp to scare the children into being good; and another old fellow said they set them up on the bank at a fishing place so the salmon would be charmed into coming close. This would be consistent with Indian thought if the right image were used. One would hardly consider eagles or bears appealing to salmon.

Tenino images.

These four stone images are six to eight inches long and were found in the Tenino country on the upper Columbia. The top line shows a turtle and mountain sheep; note the latter's backward curling horns. The bottom line shows a seal and buffalo; note the latter's triple lines carefully carved to suggest the animal's shag.

Baboon head.

This stone is one of two kinds that go under the name of baboon or monkey heads, and some think that these have been made from such a pattern. No one, however, has told us where, over the course of the years, the Indians got their baboons. Such heads are quite scarce, though there were more than a dozen of them in the collection of Frederick W. Skiff, which went to the Heye Foundation Indian Museum. This one is nine inches high, four and a half inches across the face, and six inches deep. Robert H. Miller found both the baboon and the monkey heads pictured here at the Bead Patch on the Columbia.

We have no information from the Indians about these, and I am skeptical about the baboon theory, but I do believe the head was used as a grinding stone because the scoriac lava material from which it was made is the same as that used in many of their wood-working tools. The grooves and the hand-holds are similar to other working tools. Possibly the maker assisted nature in bringing out the resemblance to an animal head.

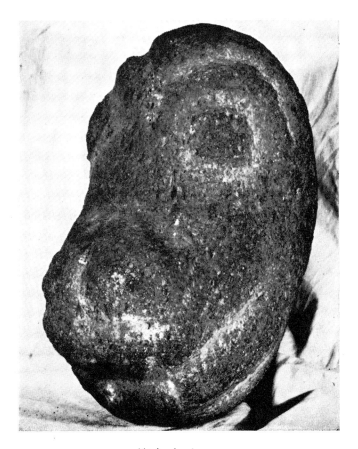

Monkey head.

This so-called monkey head is from a gravel shape that readily lends itself to a face-like carving. It seems to me that this one looks as much like a horse's head as a monkey's. Such images were easily produced by an Indian who had made perhaps a hundred or more grooved fishing sinkers. Their scarcity, though, when they could be made so easily, would indicate they were not rated highly by the Indians.

Left: Stone effigy, two feet high. **Right**: Slate carving of unknown use.

McLeod Collection
Stone artifact from the Five Mile site; probably a war club head.

Charles Hall Collection
Owl effigy mortar in the characteristic Columbia River art style, with prominent orbital ridges.

Arrowheads and Spearheads

Columbia River arrowheads and spearheads.

The picture above shows an average collection of arrowheads and spearheads from both the upper and lower Columbia River. Note the large number of very small bird points in the lower right-hand corner; these were gathered from Sauvies Island and the adjoining slough region. In the lower left-hand corner is a representative group of Calapooia Indian points from an interior small creek camp site. Note how much larger these are generally than those from the Sauvies area.

Spear or atlatl points called "bullheads."

Some finer Columbia River arrowheads.

This collection will give an idea of the delicate workmanship on the famed Columbia River arrowheads; however, it does not show the beauty of the many different stones used. Chert, agatized wood, common opal, slate, chalcedony, basalt, and green, red, and yellow jasper were all used. Even some beautiful specimens of moss agate have been picked up. Only about ten per cent of the Columbia River points were obsidian, but a little of it is found on all the camp sites. It was not handy as was the other suitable material which could be had from the river bars or from stringers in the basalt.

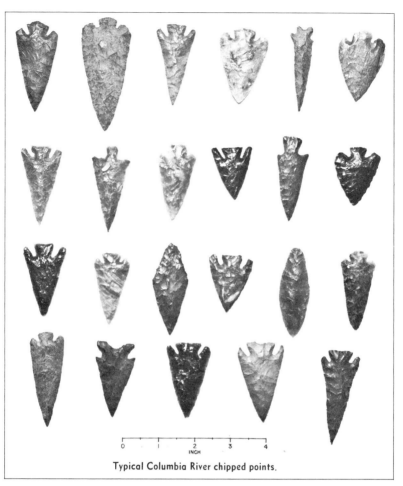

Typical Columbia River chipped points.

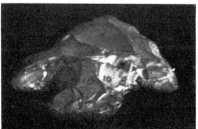

A giant arrowhead.

This is an odd piece. It is chipped to the shape of an arrowhead and is four inches in length.

Guy Gilbert of Kennewick, Washington, with part of his collection of
Columbia River artifacts.

192

Desert arrowheads and spearheads.

This is a collection showing some of the finer arrowheads and spearheads of the desert country. The two bottom pieces, as well as a couple of other large ones, have blunt sides, so I doubt that they were used as spearheads. Likely they are diggers. Several early writers spoke of Indian women digging roots with flint ends fastened to a wooden handle. I have not found any other chipped pieces that looked as appropriate as these for the work.

Desert chipped artifacts well displayed.

Obsidian war club heads.

I have found quite a few of these pointed stones of obsidian in the desert country. Those shown here are notched for a handle and seem to have served as war club heads. They would certainly have been good ones, and no stone has been found better suited to the purpose. All three of these were about six inches long. The lower one is a type of dagger, with the point chipped sharp. It was made from a spall thrown off a large piece of obsidian. The back end of this piece is cut for holding a string.

Obsidian is found in many places in central Oregon, sometimes in the form of gravel. In a few places, a butte or a small hill is made up of it. Glass Buttes in Lake County take their name from the obsidian or volcanic glass scattered over their slopes. They rise about two thousand feet above the surrounding plain, just south of Central Oregon Highway.

Desert knives made from obsidian.

194

Desert Drills and Awls

Many types of drilling, punching, and reaming pieces have been discovered in the desert country. Note the sharp, pointed chipped pieces in the upper right corner; some say they are arrowheads, but I call them punches or drills. For convenience in carrying them, a thong was tied to the notched back end. These pieces are best studied with a magnifying glass.

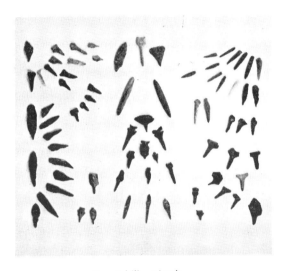

Desert drills and awls.

In the lower right corner of this picture is a specimen with a point on each end, which would preclude its use as an arrowhead. There are two interesting drills near the center of the picture, both with a notched end. A thong could be tied into this end or a handle inserted to be used in the bowstring, or up and down drilling method. I assume the broad-back ended drills were held in the hand.

Crescents, Drills, and Knives

In the lower right corner of this picture is a group of "crescents," which I have found to be most plentiful along the shoreline of dried-up Silver Lake. They have also been found on the camp sites throughout Fort Rock Valley, and along the Columbia River.

Crescents, drills, and knives.

Once an Indian on the Columbia told me that they were used as outlines for figures painted on hides. I have seen similar figures so painted, yet I feel that such a use must have been casual. Too many have been picked up for me to believe this theory to be true. Considering the places they have been found, I believe they are a type of fish knife. Still, the cutting edge is very blunt on many of them.

In the center of this same picture, next to the bottom line, is a rare little figure with notches on the side, and it is quite thin. This was an Indian "baby minder." When a papoose was left in its cradle, a bent switch was placed at the head to bring the end above the baby's face. Two or more of these pieces were tied together, dangling from their centers in such a manner that the least movement caused them to strike together to make a tinkling noise. The same principle is used in Japanese wind bells.

Fossil Lake Arrowheads and Others

Fossil Lake in central Oregon is a country where ninety-nine per cent of all chipped work is of obsidian. Near the lake is a series of sand dunes a mile wide and ten miles long. The wind over the dunes eddies ahead of them and eats a pit out of the original ground, sometimes two to four feet deep; such a pit can be seen in the picture of Fountain Bar. The six arrow points shown here were found in these pits and among the fossil bones so common in the region.

A varied collection.

An interesting feature of these points is the curvature or swelling of the sides; also the fact that four of the six are not made of obsidian though they were in obsidian country. Such finds are worth some thought. I could not tell how deep they may have been in the ground before the wind dug the pits. Fossil bones are found at all depths.

At the left is a petrified wood knife, commonly used along the river, but inclined to split with the grain. At the bottom is a seed beater; two twigs are bound together with grass. To obtain seed, a basket was held beneath the ripened grasses, and the heads were stripped off the reed stalks between the two sticks. This beater was taken from a cave in central Oregon. In the dry, alkaline dust of the overhang caves, buried objects never get wet, hence they last for ages.

The little plug at the top right was used on a salmon spear; these are common along the river. The chipped piece at the right is from the coast. It has a long,sharp, chipped edge which was used in opening shellfish.

The two horn pieces puzzled me for a long time. They are three to four inches long and the ends are blunt. I asked a very old Indian friend about them. He just grunted, took one of the pieces in his right hand, touched it to the palm of his left, and made a few imaginary lines across his face. It was a brush for putting on paint.

Scrapers

Next to arrowheads and perhaps knives, scrapers are the most common of the chipped artifacts, and they are of many types. Some are made by chipping down a thick piece of the material, while others are made from the flakes thrown off large pieces. The types, however, are much the same, no matter on which camp site they are found. Shown in this picture at the bottom left are flake scrapers notched for handles, while at the extreme right are two with notched edges as though used to make small

Various types of scrapers.

grooves or to smooth small sticks. Many of these scrapers are fine specimens, the workmanship being as good as on arrowheads. In fact, wherever you find arrowheads, you have a good chance of finding scrapers. One type, called the duckbill scraper, seems to be found over most of the world. Because there were so many of them, they must have had many important uses.

Near the center of the bottom line is a rare piece about an inch across which is definitely a "type," as I have seen several of them. They do not appear to be scrapers since they are chipped on both sides of the working edge, and they were probably used in a handle. They would be good for making a notch or groove in wood or bone.

All these chipped pieces are scrapers except the three in the upper right corner; these are drills.

Obsidian scrapers and knives.

Scrapers are not confined to the fairly small size shown here; I have picked up some that are nearly four inches across and an inch thick.

The objects on the four corners and the large center piece would be called large scrapers. The other pieces give an idea of the common shapes and sizes of the best obsidian knives.

Gougers and Chipping Stones

All of the objects pictured here are rather rare implements. The first three in *Row 1* are from the Columbia River and are made from materials commonly used there. The three just below them in *Row 2* are duplicates of them but from the desert country; they are obsidian. Though these six pieces are often considered rough arrowheads, they are really a distinct type of gouger. The working end is frequently combined with a drill; that is, the handle end of the drill is made into this kind of gouger.

Rare implements.

The three pieces to the right in *Row 1* are from the Columbia River, and the three just below, from the desert. I have found nearly a hundred of this curious implement, but have had to base my judgment of its use on inference only. The working edge is the long, rounding one. I consider it to be a wood-working tool

200

because the chipping is alternate, leaving a saw-like edge similar to a Columbia River saw rock. Also, the chipping is too coarse to be used in working on bone or horn. It is a handy tool for cutting a groove in any size of wood piece.

The three pieces to the left in *Row* 3 are of fine-grained basalt. I have found them in the desert country and in the Tualatin Plains, about ten miles west of Portland in Calapooia country. The museum at the city hall in Portland has a tray of very similarly shaped stones marked "sling stones from New Hebrides." The size, shape, and kind of stone are so much like those in the illustration that I doubt if I could separate them from those of a desert collection, if they were mixed. However, I do not believe they were used as sling stones in this area because I know of no record of Indians in this region using slings. Besides, no Indian here would put so much work on a stone that would be lost the first time it was shot. Too, some of these stones are flat and thin and would not be satisfactory as sling stones; and many are too light in weight to be effective as a weapon.

In my opinion, these three pieces were chipping stones used in making the larger or, perhaps, cruder articles. They could also have been employed as the middle tool utilized in the process of making finer articles. My inferences are based on experiment. Try one on a piece of obsidian, and you will soon find that it will "take hold." Those shaped like the ones in the picture are simply the few that have been so "improved." Those roughly shaped are commonly found about the large piles of chippings, constituting what we call "work shops." I have come across as many as eight of them together, like eggs in a basket, alongside a large pile of flakes or chippings—apparently just as the workers left them. The fact is, I have the only improved ones I know of, more than a dozen of them; and they vary from two to three inches in length.

The three pieces to the right in *Row* 3 are atlatl weights. They vary from two to four inches and all have one flat side and grooves at the ends for attachment to the throwing stick. All three are of polished gravel. It is quite probable that the small one was either a child's atlatl or a stone used for ceremonial purposes.

Pipes

Pipes.

Western Indians developed many variations of both the tube and elbow types of pipes. Though they were made of many materials, the stone ones are the only ones that have survived in any great number. Some of the Columbia River pipes are particularly beautiful specimens, many of them highly ornamented, and some so heavy an Indian almost had to lie down to smoke one of them. The tube pipe and the funnel pipe in the top line are from the Columbia; the others are from the desert country, where I have found the heaviest pieces.

At the left are cloud-blower pipes; to the right, a wine-glass pipe and a tubular type.

Typical Columbia River tube pipes. The one on the right is the wine-glass type.

Pipes from Wakemap Mound.

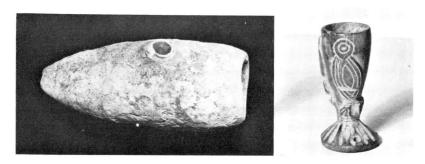

Left: cloud-blower pipe, one of the earliest types, found near The Dalles. It has a hole in the side as well as at the stem. Cloud blowers were not smoked; the lighted end was pressed to the lips and the smoke blown about the room. *Right:* Carved stone pipe, found at the Leachman site.

Bone Implements

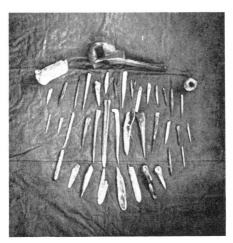

Bone artifacts.

Bone needles for fine sewing were scraped to a very sharp point; whereas large, blunt-pointed needles were used in making tule mats. The heavy, blunt end of the pieces shown in the bottom line above were used as a finishing tool in fine chipping work.

In the upper right and upper left of this picture are pieces of hollowed bone or horn used as handles for knives. The top center piece is a knife scabbard made from the knee joint of an elk. A knife with a hilt or a thick handle will drop down into it but not go clear through. The right side of the scabbard is notched to fasten to a belt. The end of the other side bears a fairly-good carving of a bear. If you look at the picture sideways from the right, you can plainly see the bear. Such decoration may be rather modern in conception.

Elkhorn wedges.　　　　　　　*Woodcock Collection*

Bone Implements. Top, harpoon; center, awl; bottom, needles.

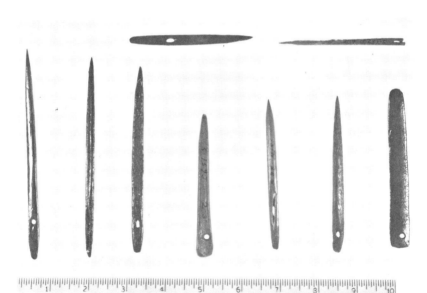

Bone needles. If they do not have an eye, they are called awls.

Wood Carvings

Ash burl cooking bowl.

The Indians of both the upper and the lower river used these wooden cooking bowls made from burls cut from ash or maple trees. After several years of use for cooking, such vessels took on an odor which was far from pleasant to civilized noses. The very old one shown here is quite rare; it came from Sauvies Island a long time ago. A few may be had from some of the reservation Indians, but no more will be picked up on the camp sites.

Wooden salmon club.

Sieberg Collection

If there is any significance to these carved wooden sticks, I have not been able to discover it. To get information from an old Indian, you have to show him what you are talking about, but even doing this I failed to get an explanation. As nearly as I can make out, these sticks, as well as the carved-board images, are

Carved sticks.

just objects which the Indians put up about their homes. When they are found about a grave, they signify a mark of respect.

The center object between the sticks was dug out of a camp site near Skamania; it is not ancient because it has saw and nail marks. The carving was done by burning and scraping, and it was originally painted as marks of red still show.

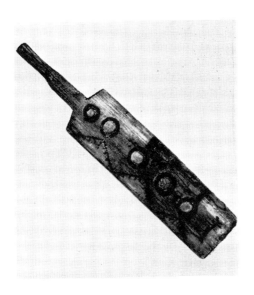

Wooden Indian fan.

When I asked a group of bright old Indians what this wood carving was, they talked among themselves a little, then one who could speak pretty good English said,

"A fan. Injun get hot just like white man." When asked what the carving meant, he pointed to the animal at the end of the fan and said,

"This an elk." Pointing to the zigzag line, he said,

"This the mountains, and these dots mean more elk. This man tells us he was great hunter, killed lots of elk all over the mountains." Touching the circles below the zigzag line, he went on,

"He say he great warrior; he take five scalps; these two, long hair, they Injun; these three, no hair, they white man." Then, one of the old fellows among those who had remained sitting, looked up and said,

"I bet you him big liar."

These two wood carvings at the right are rare representatives of an art that was practiced throughout the Northwest. Lewis and Clark, as well as several of the early immigrants, speak of the number of these figures about vault burial houses on the north bank near what is now North Bonneville. The two shown were found by the late Henry J. Biddle in 1906, under the easterly overhang of Beacon Rock. Some of these carvings were more than a foot wide, and, in addition to human beings, they also represented birds, animals, fish, and various imaginary figures. Because wood decays, burns, and floats, there is little likelihood of many of these carvings coming to light.

Note the hat on the left figure; this is interesting and informative. Hats were extensively used on the lower Columbia and were usually made of grass.

I hope some specimens of this rare work found their way to eastern museums in the early days, since so little was saved here.

Wilke Collection

Wooden bowl.

Wood carvings found at Beacon Rock.

Personal Adornment Artifacts

Before the coming of the white men, the Indians made articles for personal adornment that were of enduring materials; therefore we can still find them on the camp sites. They consisted of wampum, as shown in the two perpendicular strings; hiaqua shells, as shown at the extreme right; stone beads, a few of which are shown; stone rings, which are very rare; and stone pendants of many shapes. The pendants were sometimes made of pieces of shell or of chipped material. Any small object which the Indians could perforate, they would hang on themselves.

Personal adornment artifacts.

Feather work and porcupine quill adornments are gone, naturally, except from some well-protected places. Caves along the rivers of northern Oregon are all in basalt rock and are thus always full of seams that let in the rain. Because nothing has been preserved in them, we must look to such places as the caves of central and southeastern Oregon for very old material.

George H. Himes, long-time curator of the Oregon Historical Society, and one of its founders in 1898, stands beside model of an old Indian canoe—made by Indians but using white man's tools.

Mr. Miller and his "canoe."

In the foreground is a hollowed log which the veteran relic hunter, Robert H. Miller, rescued from a large drift on Sauvies Island. At first he thought it might be an Indian woman's work canoe; now he is inclined to believe it is a horse trough.

Petroglyphs near Vantage, Washington, that are now drowned by the Wanapum dam.

Part Five

PETROGLYPHS AND PICTOGRAPHS

IN MY EXPLORATIONS AS A RELIC HUNTER FOR OVER HALF A century, in addition to large quantities of chipped artifacts and stone work, I have found a considerable number of petroglyphs and pictographs. Petroglyphs are stone carvings, the name being taken from the Greek *petros* (stone) plus *glyphe* (carving). Pictographs are paintings on stone, and take their name from the Latin *pictus* (painted) plus *graphicus* (writing).

Along the Columbia River the petroglyphs are far more numerous than the pictographs, though many are now covered by the backed-up waters of the great dams. The reason for the lack of pictographs, especially on the lower river, is the absence of suitable rock faces to work upon. Such cliffs as exist are of fractured basalt. In a measure, carved images replaced the petroglyphs where the river banks became clay or gravel. Many of these images have been found about Sauvies Island, while some of the best pictographs occur in the desert country east of the Cascades.

The carvings are found as far downstream as Fishers Landing, or about nine miles above Vancouver, and there are a few at Oregon City. The largest collection of petroglyphs I know of was on the Washington side of the Columbia, about a mile east of the railroad station of Spearfish, but the site is now under water. This concentration is easily accounted for because it was near the permanent settlement of Wishram.

Westward from Wishram and paralleling the highway, the Paha Cliffs, perpendicular walls of lava rock, are not remarkable for height, but are of such regularity and symmetry that they seem to have been carved by human hands. Indian legends state that Speelyei, the coyote god, created the many pillars of stone by turning mortals and beasts into rock. Geologists say that seismic and volcanic action raised the mountain area, and river erosion left the odd-shaped formations.

The bedrock flats of Celilo, now flooded, are also spotted over with carvings on both sides of the river. Below Celilo at Seufert, many Indian petroglyphs and pictographs were once visible on the bluffs facing the Columbia. Prehistoric as well as historic aborigines of the region came here to fish for salmon; and while some of the pictures of fishes, beavers, elks, water dogs, and men were doubtless made as primitive art expression, others were carved and painted to carry messages.

One of the most famous petroglyphs is on a rock farther up the Columbia, in the vicinity of East Wenatchee, Washington. This rock bears thousand-year-old petroglyphs and crude aboriginal carvings, now barely visible. Before Rock Island Dam was built, numerous rocks with petroglyphs could be seen on islands in the river. Hundreds of rock carvings on Whale Island, in Washington, are now covered by the waters of Priest Rapids dam.

On the Washington side of the Snake River, near Asotin, Buffalo Rock projects from the scarred cliffs of the eastern canyon wall. Here are a number of pictographs on the low rocks near the river's edge. Most of the drawings represent men, with huge, square shoulders, short legs, and horned headdresses; others resemble mountain sheep, deer, and elk. According to an explanation advanced by the Smithsonian Institution, these pictographs were made by the Basket Maker Indians some three thousand years ago.

Near Rogersburg, Washington, close to the junction of the Snake and Grande Ronde rivers there is also a rock where Indian pictographs are still visible, although decades of weathering have dimmed their sharp outlines. Some of the drawings are easily decipherable. One, a petroglyph, is a carving of two men with flint knives engaged in mortal combat. Others show men, horses, and mountain sheep. And, west of Yakima, in the Naches River Valley, there is a basalt cliff with some very old Indian paintings. Legends of the Yakimas say that they were there before their own tribes came to live in this land.

Another excellent site for observing pictographs is in Picture Gorge, a deep cleft through which the John Day River in Oregon pours its foaming torrent. The defile is so narrow that even in summer its depths are shadowed and gloomy. Stratified, crumbling basalt cliffs rear to a height of five hundred feet. The prehistoric pictographs that give the gorge its name are on a comparatively smooth stretch of lava wall at an angle facing east. Scientists state that the crude markings, painted in red oxide, have been there fifty to eighty centuries. No satisfactory interpretation of their symbolism has ever been advanced. They are about three feet above the ground, but their weathered dullness makes them obscure. On the rugged bluffs of Dry River in central Oregon is another collection of good, though age-dimmed, pictographs.

Throughout the sagebrush section of central and southwestern Oregon are many groups of pictures. A much larger percentage of these are pictographs than on the Columbia River, and they are quite different, appearing to be more in the nature of a real sign writing. It is a known fact that desert Indians were far advanced in the use of signs—that they could leave their markings along their trail, on bare ground or in the sand, which would be understood by their people following behind. On the Klamath Reservation, I have talked with several old Indians of these desert tribes. Near Abert Lake and at the base of Hart Mountain, in southeast Oregon, there are excellent examples of prehistoric painting and carving.

As the dams took their toll of the many petroglyphs along the Columbia, an extremely small portion of the carvings were cut from the solid rock and transferred to museums; many more were photographed, often with chalk added to clarify the outlines. A number of these petroglyphs appear later in these pages, among them some of the carvings from around Roosevelt, Washington on the upper river, past Fountain Bar.

I do not know of any white man who can interpret these petroglyphs, but I do know of old Indians who seemed to understand many of them quite well. From my own study of them, I have concluded that they can be divided generally into several types:

1. Pictures carved as expressions of art.

2. Water devils that are grotesque representations of imaginary animals. These are generally found near the water and in places from which it is dangerous to fish. The old Indians will tell you that at such a place a bad spirit holds forth in the waters below, and it will try to draw you in. These figures no doubt do cause a fisherman to be careful. One Indian said, "They scare children away from bad places." Many of these characters appear very old, and many are deeply carved. Possibly some of the figures that suggest water devils were meant to be lizards, the patron animal of some family. As time has stained them the color of the cliffs on which they were done, it is necessary to chalk them in to photograph them.

3. Carvings that attempt to tell a story. There are a few of these that give, perhaps, an adventure of the artist, or maybe a chapter from one of the long stories used to pass away the winter evenings.

4. Suns, or sections of concentric circles, which could be parts of suns. These are found rather frequently along the Columbia and must have some connection with death because many of them mark graves. It has been claimed that they indicate sun worship, but I have never found any sign of it. Often they are paintings rather than carvings, though sometimes they are painted carvings.

5. A picture of a bird or an animal that was the patron of some Indian family. Call it a crest or coat of arms, or what you like. It was sometimes used to mark the family's fishing place. The rich Indians owned the good places, and the poor ones had to rustle their fish wherever they could.

Besides these classifications, there are along the river many individual figures, or small groups, that are difficult to understand. Perhaps the best known petroglyph on the Columbia and the most elaborate, is a combination of carving and painting at the old village of Wishram. The Indians call it Tsagaglalal. It is a pair of eyes about six feet high and looks down upon the old trail that passed along there. The Indians will tell you, "She sees you come and she sees you go." Give this what interpretation you like. Perhaps it means a passerby should watch his step. Or, if he sees something he would like to steal, he should just forget it, because she has her eye on him. The carving must have been quite brilliant when new, but the red paint is pretty well worn off now.

Tsagaglalal—"She Who Watches."

Certain figures such as eyes, ribs, suns, four-pointed stars, and zigzag lines appear over and over again, but the "Eyes of Tsagaglalal" are likely the most famous. The top picture is an elaborate example. Note the eyes watching the bearded figure, and the little water devil. Both pictures have three pairs of eyes.

Petroglyphs at a fishing place.

An old Indian's interpretation of this carving may be of interest. It is on a bedrock boulder at a very dangerous fishing place.
The cliff drops straight down to boiling water. The fisherman
must stand with one foot out upon a projecting point of rock to
use his dipnet. The right top figure in the carving and the
second from left on the bottom are easily recognized as water
devils, warning you to be careful.

The bottom left represents a man's chest, heart, and lungs.
They are a warning that a man must be strong and steady to fish
here. The old Indian pounded his chest as he explained. At the
lower right is an arrangement of the sun and moon, which means
that this is a good fishing place late in the afternoon or at night.
During the day the sun strikes the water in such a way that the
fish can see the fisherman and shy off. The mountain sheep in
the carving are only background pictures, or perhaps a family
crest.

Suns and partial suns.

Water devil.

Weird characters such as this are found generally near the water and in places from which it is dangerous to fish. The Indians call them "water devils." A bad spirit holds forth in the deep waters below them. One Indian said, "They scare children away from bad places."

This figure appears very old; time has stained it the color of the cliff on which it was done. Many such figures are deeply carved.

Petroglyph Canyon.

The low cliffs overlooking the river, just east of The Dalles, have been called Petroglyph Canyon because of the myriad carvings there. Now all are buried under the waters of Lake Celilo except the few preserved by the National Park Service, The Dalles Museum Commission, and whatever was picked up by individuals. This petroglyph from the canyon shows a typical Spedis Owl, a water devil or lizard, and a four-pointed star, along with what are apparently random carvings.

Full-stone petroglyphs.

Here entire stones have been converted to petroglyph use. At the top is the well-known piggy-back fish from The Dalles area; and below is the frog or turtle effigy at Fishers above Vancouver, Washington. The white lines were marked on to show the deepest incisions.

227

Monolith from Wallula.

Close-up of another famous stone with all-over carvings—the huge monolith at the Portland City Hall, shown earlier with the old-time Indians.

Near The Dalles.

Top: This large head with rays — now toppled over — was found on an island in the Columbia near The Dalles. It has a strong Mayan influence; some suggest that wandering Yucatans may have roamed this far.

Bottom: This rare peaked-hat figure with the profile nose was found on the Oregon side of the Columbia near The Dalles.

Upstream to spawn?

The coyote in the upper picture was likely a family sign. The lower picture has been variously interpreted. One interesting theory is that it shows a female salmon going upstream to spawn during a seasonal run. The marks at the right indicate the length of the run, thirty-seven days—thirty and seven; while the figure above the numbers marks the site of an Indian village.

Hunting and fishing petroglyphs.

Top: This story petroglyph is at the mouth of the John Day River. Here is a hunter drawing his arrow at a goat or mountain sheep and a man with a dipnet containing one salmon.

Bottom: In this hunting scene a man is pursuing four elk or mountain sheep with the help of three dogs. The lower carvings show a linear figure and a lizard. This work was done at Roosevelt, Washington, an area rich in petroglyphs.

Spedis Owls look out on Petroglyph Canyon.

The irrepressible Spedis Owl occurs in several areas, but some of the best are in Petroglyph Canyon. Here he appears twice, along with elk and a group of mountain sheep. Note the excellent game tracks to the left of the lower Spedis.

Story-telling, cliff-top carvings.

Not all carvings are on the face of cliffs. These are on the flat tops of cliffs just east of Roosevelt, Washington. Both pictures show petroglyphs that attempt to tell a story.

Near Tenino.

A lively-looking little petroglyph on the cliffs east of Tenino, and a view of the old fishwheel in the same area.

Some Indian geometry.

The carvings in the lower picture are rare examples of geo-metric carvings found at Tenino, Washington. The character at the extreme left is Seaman. At the top is an elaborate specimen of the water devil, or lizard.

Top: Elk pictograph at Big Eddy. *Bottom:* Sheep and "Name it yourself."

Though sheep often served merely as background pictures, they dominate these petroglyphs at the John Day Bar. One interesting theory about the many sheep effigies is that they were carved simply from their elusiveness and the Indians' desire to obtain them; animals valuable both for their meat and skin. On the other hand, fish, their staple food, were rarely pictured, possibly because they were so easily caught.

Elk and others.

Men on horseback.

Petroglyphs near Cliffs, Washington.

The top picture, near Cliffs, Washington, gives an idea of how crowded with petroglyphs some of the cliffs along the Columbia are. The bottom picture shows the variety of petroglyphs found there.

Left: Water devil near Wishram. *Right*: Petroglyphs near Blalock, Oregon.

Hunting scene at Blalock.

Carvings in Petroglyph Canyon near the Long Narrows, now drowned by The Dalles dam.

Tule Lake petroglyphs.

There are some long rows of petroglyphs in Tule Lake in Klamath County, Oregon. The lake was reclaimed with the diversion of the waters of Lost River, but when these carvings were made it was either during a dry cycle, or they were made from a canoe. The chief interest of these pictures is the number of them, partly accounted for by the softness of the sandstone cliff. They could be scraped in easily with but little pecking. This picture shows a spot not far from Bloody Point, where the Modoc Indians waylaid and murdered a train of immigrants in 1852.

Desert pictographs.

These are examples of paintings found in the desert country of central Oregon, which seem very close to sign writing. They were not simply signs of direction; they told a story, and a large number of the characters were repeated many miles apart.

Faceted beads . . . These generally range from a quarter-inch to three-quarters inch.
Many of the larger ones are a rich, dark blue and have been found on Russian sites in
Alaska—hence they are often referred to as Russian beads.

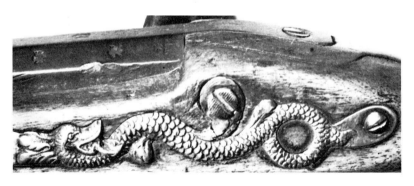

Serpent sideplate on a Northwest gun. The Indians would not buy this gun without
the serpent.

Part Six

TRADE GOODS

THE ARTICLES SHOWN HERE ARE OLD, AS TRADE GOODS GO; AND they give a good idea of the kind of stuff the Indians got for the furs they sold to the traders, the trappers, and the explorers. Some of these items came from an old burial place at the Lower Cascades; vaults that were described by Lewis and Clark and were in use long after their time; in fact, until about 1860.

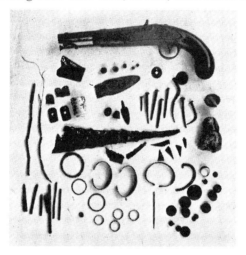

Early-day trade goods.

Handmade nails, several of which appear here, were priced at one nail for one beaver skin. The old pistol at the top of the picture came from a grave on Beacon Rock. At the left are cylindrical beads which had been rolled from pieces of sheet copper, materials that the Indians prized highly. From them they also made finger rings, copper bracelets, and other items. Part of an original sheet of metal is shown in the center; this and the three small pieces below it were found together on a camp site. The Indians had cut the pieces off with their stone tools to make metal arrowheads. All four pieces were found lying on a flat boulder with a couple of round stones, presumably hammers, apparently just as their owners had left them.

In the lower right-hand corner are several broadhead tacks from some immigrant's leather-bound trunk; and at the extreme right center is the porcelain head of a dog, which, if it were complete, would certainly be a collectors' item.

Hudson's Bay Company axe—a popular trade item.

Hand-made nail. Early blacksmiths made these from bar iron during slack time. The oval head shows the mark of the blacksmith's hammer.

An early Hudson's Bay Company beaver trap, highly prized by both whites and Indians.

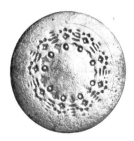 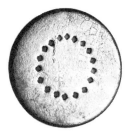 

Colonial buttons—another popular trade item. Such metal buttons were manufactured in the North American colonies as early as 1706.

Lewis and Clark peace medal. These medals were given out by the explorers to prominent Indian chiefs.

Metal arrow points. Metal in any form was for many years the most valuable item of trade.

Trade Beads

A large part of the so-called Indian or trade beads were of the small size and no different from those found in present-day stores. We do find, however, many kinds of larger beads from a half inch to an inch in length. Some of these are perhaps no longer made. The finest among them are the ones called Venetian or Inlaid Venetian; they are rare and beautiful.

The beads most interesting, historically, are the Oriental or Chinese; the minute you see one of these, you immediately know it by its color and shape. They were brought to the Northwest by the early ships trading off the coast. These traders, whether from our east coast or from Europe, went first to China, where their cargo was sold. In China, they purchased what seemed suitable for the Indian trade, including, naturally, beads which were the one principal article used. After getting what furs they could from the Indians, they went back to China, disposed of their pelts, and took on a load of tea, silk, and other items for their home country. If they were fortunate, this changing cargo made the voyage highly profitable.

Evidence indicates that the beads were made in Italy and shipped to China, the source of supply for the trading ships. The Russian beads are so-called because the Russians also bought and used them for trade. They have been found all along the Northwest Coast, but they occur most frequently on old village sites in Alaska.

Chevron beads similar to this were made of polychrome glass arranged in layers. The outer layer was either blue or green and the ends—usually red and white—formed a star pattern of about twelve points.

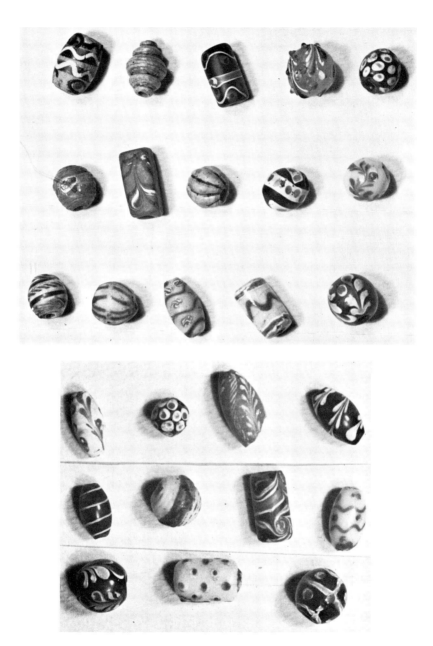

Polychrome beads like these date back to about 1800. Many have been found on gravesites at Upper and Lower Memaloose islands. The inlaid type were made by hand and no two were exactly alike.

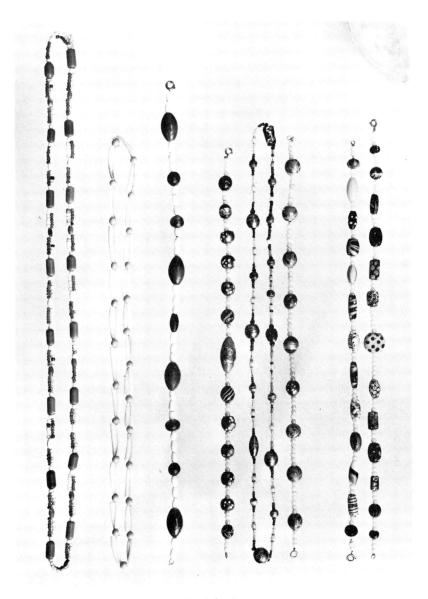

Trade beads.

These beads are not found strung as shown here, but are usually picked up one at a time from the sand.

Phoenix Buttons

Many kinds of buttons have been found, some of which are quite interesting; but among the most curious are the numbered buttons picked up mainly along the Columbia. These are the Phoenix buttons, so named because of their "rising from fire" design. The French phrase describing the Phoenix bird which appears on the buttons (*Je renais de mes cendres*) is translated as "I rise again from my ashes." It is a symbol of eternal youth and immortality, of death and resurrection, and has been used by both Pagan and Christian civilizations since ancient times.

To the Arabians it is a fabulous bird, the only one of its kind, that is said to live a certain number of years, at the close of which it makes a nest of spices, sings a melodious dirge, flaps its wings to set fire to the pile, burns itself to ashes, and comes forth with new life, to repeat the former one.

The Egyptians believed the Phoenix was sacred to the sun

Phoenix buttons.

god and that it made its nest in the Temple of the Sun. Because of the bird's association with alchemy, it was adopted as a sign over chemists' shops. Though the periods between the transformations of the Phoenix are generally supposed to be five hundred years, they are sometimes estimated as high as fifteen hundred years.

As a result of inquiries made at the Hudson's Bay Company in London, and extensive correspondence with eastern authorities, I feel certain that the Phoenix buttons were not known to the Bay Company. From my readings of the records of early travelers to the Northwest, it seems probable that the buttons were brought here by Nathaniel Wyeth, an ambitious business man of Boston, who planned a salmon-packing industry on Sauvies Island, and came prepared for business with a large assortment of trading goods. It is significant that the majority of these buttons have been found within transportation distance of his headquarters at Fort William on the island.

It can be ascertained that the buttons were here before 1835 because a number were found on the site of Sauvies' Multnomah Village, which by that time had been totally destroyed by fire. Wyeth's first trip to the Columbia, in 1832, ended unsuccessfully with the loss of his ship; but he returned in 1834 to organize the Columbia River Fishing and Trading Company. This trip, too, ended in failure and Wyeth went back to Boston to re-enter the ice business in which he had been successful earlier.

It seems plausible that Wyeth, who shipped ice to the West Indies prior to coming to the Oregon Country, might have obtained the buttons, and many of the uniforms they once adorned, in exchange for his valuable commodity; well aware that they would be highly valuable in his long-planned Oregon venture. The buttons are similar to those appearing on regimental uniforms of Henri Christophe, King of Haiti from 1811 till 1820. All the Phoenix buttons bear the number of a regiment of infantry, artillery, or of cavalry. King Christophe used this emblem on his own crown and coat of arms, as well as on the uniforms of his men.

In any case, the buttons, and the uniforms they identified, had not been delivered to Christophe before a paralytic stroke destroyed his power and he ended his life with a silver bullet. Though the buttons have been reported chiefly from fishing areas along the Columbia, they have been picked up elsewhere in the Northwest; one is even reported from southern California. Wyeth must have brought a large supply of them.

Okoke Opoots

INDEX

253